HOUSE
STYLE

HOUSE
STYLE

*Inspirational styles and designs
for your home*

LORRIE MACK

INTRODUCTION BY SUSAN COLLIER

This edition published by
Macdonald Illustrated, a division of
Macdonald & Co (Publishers) Ltd.,
165 Great Dover Street, London SE1 4YA.

A CIP catalogue record for this book is available
from the British Library.

ISBN 0 356 20270 4

Author's acknowledgements
I am particularly grateful to Jenny Jones,
who conceived the original idea for this
book. Special thanks also to my editor,
Gillian Prince, and my agent, Barbara
Levy, for their support and encouragement;
and to Penny David, for her knowledgeable
and accurate copy editing.

This edition first published
for Marks & Spencer plc in 1989
by Macdonald & Co (Publishers) Ltd
London & Sydney

A member of Maxwell Pergamon
Publishing Corporation plc
66-73 Shoe Lane, London EC4P 4AB

Typeset by Flairplan Phototypesetting
Ltd, Ware, Hertfordshire
Printed and bound in Italy by
OFSA SpA, Milan

Editor: Gillian Prince
Text editor: Penny David
Art director: Bobbie Colgate-Stone
Designer: Sheila Volpe
Picture researcher: Amanda Baker
Senior production controller: Sonya
Sibbons

Special photography by
John Hollingshead
Stylist: Sue Russell

CONTENTS

INTRODUCTION

There's never been a better time for experimenting with interior design: endless inspiration is all around us, some exciting – some confusing. For a comprehensive and instant reference source, this book will be invaluable. Finding your own sense of style can be, above all, fun, as you learn to understand and appreciate the qualities of light, colour, pattern, texture and space which determine the atmosphere of your home. Of course, other considerations such as the size and proportions of the space you want to decorate, your budget, and the people with whom you share your life, must be taken into account as well, so that you arrive at a home which is not only practical and efficient, but also comfortable and sympathetic – particularly to you. This lavishly illustrated and clearly written book will help to guide you along the way. Use it, with its sound advice and enormous range of interior design possibilities, as a good companion on the exciting journey of discovery towards your personal synthesis of style.

Susan Collier.

STARTING OUT

First and foremost, a home should be a comfortable and efficient place to live in, but most of us want our rooms to fulfil more than practical functions – we expect them to look attractive and stylish as well, not just to impress other people, but to provide the pleasant and sympathetic domestic environment we all need in order to escape from the world and recharge our batteries.

Unfortunately, though, wanting beautiful surroundings and having the ability to achieve them are not the same thing; like any other skill, creating successful decorating schemes involves knowledge and practice, but it also needs something else – visual awareness, or a kind of educated eye for what is well designed and appropriate for you and your home. When it comes to fashion, most of us have acquired a working degree of this awareness; we're used to shopping for clothes and can quickly identify garments that suit us. We buy furnishings far less often, however, and can easily become bewildered by the range of styles available.

If you're faced with furnishing a whole home, or even a single room, and feel unsure about your own taste and needs, don't make any major decisions or purchases until you develop a little more confidence. Start by looking at as many interiors and furnishings as possible – in books and magazines, in films and on television, in museums and stately homes, and in furnishing shops and catalogues. Without trying to reach any conclusions, begin to pick out the looks that hold the most appeal. After a time you'll find that many of these have common elements: they're all cosy and cluttered, for example, or cool and stark. It may be that one colour, or one family of colours (pastel, primary), keeps attracting you, or even just the atmosphere of a particular period or country. The more influences you explore, the more quickly you will get a

LEFT This delightfully traditional room embodies the three most important qualities you should strive for in any design scheme: comfort, efficiency and a pleasing appearance. The plump, well-cushioned sofa provides greater-than-average comfort; the skilfully arranged furnishings leave traffic paths where they're most logical; and the collection of beautiful and well-loved objects is set off against simple cream walls, and highlighted by sunlight streaming in through delicate lace curtains.

firm idea of what you like.

In searching for a style to develop, remember that it must do more than suit your own taste. It must also be appropriate for your home, so don't try to re-create a grand country house if you live in two poky rooms, or a Mediterranean villa if there's not much light. More than this, your chosen idiom has to suit your life: if your household includes elderly people, or small children and animals, a ruthlessly minimalist scheme is not for you. Finally, be realistic about your budget. If Victorian opulence is your fantasy and money is tight, either go for a more modest look, or accept the fact that your rooms will have to grow into their chosen look very gradually indeed. In any case, and especially when you move into a new home, don't try to do everything at once; live in the place for a while to get a feeling for its space and light, then begin to add furnishings and decorative details slowly, as you discover things you really love. This cautious approach not only prevents expensive mistakes, it also guards against the sterile, soulless, showroom atmosphere that instantly created rooms sometimes have.

This book will help you to find a style that works for you, and to adapt it for use in your own home, even if you don't live in a thatched cottage or a Provençal farmhouse; it is essentially a collection of decorating ideas that give a general feeling or impression, rather than a set of rules on how to re-create a particular period or look with academic accuracy. Use the sections in this way, to give a subtle flavour to your schemes, or as jumping-off points from which to explore one particular style in more detail. You might find it easiest to stick to the same basic idiom for all your rooms, but if you want to vary them, at least keep the moods related – a country-cottage bedroom would work well with a Victorian living room, whereas a high-tech bathroom beside an eastern-bazaar-

ABOVE *Let your taste in small objects and accessories act as a guide when you're contemplating an entire design scheme: the owner of this flowery Victorian tinware, for example, is unlikely to feel comfortable in a stark, modernist home.*

LEFT *The influence of* ikebana, *with its emphasis on asymmetrical forms, is particularly strong in this modern treatment of a room in an Edwardian house. The sculptural forms of the triangular glass table top, its supports modelled on the shape of African beans, the spun metal chairs with woven cane seats, and the arrangements of willow and bird of paradise flowers, all contribute to the general effect.*

like bedroom would jar the senses.

Above all, remember that this is your home, and your feelings about it are more important than any other consideration. Begin cautiously, go slowly, and follow expert advice. Later, as you become more experienced, you'll gain enough confidence to break the rules, experiment with your own ideas, and create uniquely beautiful and personal rooms.

Using Colour

Colour is probably the single most important design element in your home, since it affects not only the visual appeal of your rooms, but also their apparent size and brightness, and even the way you feel in them. Because colours have such a huge influence, they should be selected with a number of criteria in mind, but the one factor you *can* ignore is fashion: you may read that peach or grey is the very latest thing, but these may be the worst possible choices for your home – and almost by definition they'll be last year's news before you want to redecorate. Here again, it's your personal preferences that count, so start by identifying the colours you're naturally drawn to; if these aren't immediately obvious, take a look at your wardrobe – the shades you choose in something as personal as clothes are bound to be ones you'll feel happy living with.

Apart from the very personal feelings that colours arouse in us, however, each colour has specific qualities of its own that affect everybody – red and orange in all their variations are stimulating, for example, whereas green makes people feel calm. Colour can even influence our perception of temperature, so that a blue room will tend to *feel* chillier than a yellow one, even if their thermostats register identical readings. To make these characteristics work for you, go for warm hues in cool, north-facing rooms and in busy areas like kitchens and

BELOW This inviting breakfast room seems to be bathed in warm, dappled light, an effect achieved by finely washing all the surfaces – skirtings, mouldings and shelves as well as walls – with a soft buttery shade of gold.

living rooms, and avoid vibrant, exciting shades like orange in your bedroom, where you need to feel relaxed. If you love strong, pure tones, use them for small accessories rather than on the walls, where they can overpower the room and its occupants. Save dramatic schemes for areas that people pass through quickly, like bathrooms or halls. Similarly, you can give a separate dining room a less subtle treatment than the one you choose for the living room, which needs a softer, more self-effacing complexion to cater for long periods of use.

The paler the floor, ceiling and walls are in any room, the larger it will look, but beware of decorating darkish rooms in pure white, since they can end up looking grey and dingy; go for one of the warm, tinted whites instead, or even a buttery cream or a flattering flesh pink tone.

Colour will help to pull a room together if you treat all the surfaces in the same way rather than picking out the ceiling in white; this is an especially useful tip when you have to cope with awkward shapes and angles. By the same token, you can camouflage an oversized piece of furniture by painting it the same colour as the walls, or covering it in a blending fabric.

Once you've taken all these things into consideration and decided what you want, guard against errors by looking at each potential purchase in the same kind of light that it will be exposed to in your home – natural illumination, or tungsten or fluorescent lamps. Finally, never try to carry a colour in your head – not even professional designers can do this; always take with you a sample of any shade you want to match or co-ordinate. (If you can't get hold of a paint or fabric swatch, try to duplicate it with a reel of sewing cotton, which is very cheap and comes in an enormous range of shades and tones.) Taking care with the details and getting them right could make all the difference between success and failure.

ABOVE To make a multi-coloured scheme work successfully, take care to provide it with plenty of neutral colour. Here, a vibrant medley of pinks, blues, greens, golds and purples is displayed against the pale backgrounds of the printed fabric and wallpaper, the white lace curtain, and the simple bleached floorboards.

COUNTRY STYLE

*T*here is something in most of us that views a pastoral existence, despite its hardships, as somehow simpler, slower and more civilized than an urban one. By taking design inspiration from this way of life, we can enjoy some of its pleasures without experiencing any of the drawbacks.

Country homes are, above all, practical: floors are hardwearing, surfaces are washable, and fussy detailing is conspicuous by its absence. Rooms are not tied to any single period or trend, since their decoration will have evolved slowly and been influenced more by the demands of rural life than the vagaries of fashion.

English Country House

Deliberately setting out to re-create an English country-house look is almost a contradiction in terms – the appeal of this style lies in the fact that it's almost completely artless and uncontrived. With their origin in the homes of landed aristocrats and prosperous farmers, such rooms are an unselfconscious blend of grandeur and informality; although the furnishings tend to be slightly worn as a result of being passed down from earlier generations, they are of excellent quality and unfailingly solid, comfortable and easy to use. The atmosphere is cosy and cluttered, yet there are few diminutive or delicate items in evidence – tables, chairs, sofas and storage pieces are crafted on a scale to match the generous proportions of the rooms, and sometimes of their affluent occupants as well. For this reason, it would be a mistake to attempt this style in very small or low rooms.

SETTING THE SCENE

The walls of country-house rooms are either plain (plaster or simple panelling), or papered with a suitably large-scale design – full-blown blooms would be a good choice, or perhaps bold stripes. The grandest halls and passages feature natural stonework, but you can get a similar effect using a *trompe-l'oeil* paint technique. The dominant colours are clear and natural without being garish – leaf green and sky blue are examples – and are set off by large expanses of off-white, warm cream, or subtle pastels like primrose yellow or eau-de-nil. There is a profusion of pattern and colour, but nothing is matched or co-ordinated perfectly, and the furniture (mahogany, dark oak or walnut, never pine) is set out in relaxed groups rather than arranged in stiff, symmetrical formations.

Ideally, the floor will be of first-quality timber, lovingly waxed, then covered with a huge and priceless oriental carpet, but in the absence of such luxuries, consider

RIGHT *Give your home a country-garden feeling by choosing clear, fresh colour schemes and adding massed bunches of flowers – printed on fabrics, woven into rugs, and painted on walls and furniture.*

- When mixing patterns, don't try to match colours exactly, but do stick to those with the same intensity, so that delicate pastel designs are not overpowered by those in deep, rich tones like claret and navy. Patterns need not have precisely the same scale either, but again, don't use very tiny motifs with huge overpowering ones. Having built up an arrangement of richly layered patterns, provide relief for the eye in the form of a large area of plain colour near by.

- Coir matting is cheap and hardwearing, but like all natural fibres, it may shrink or stretch slightly in use. To avoid problems, buy and cut out a little more than you need for each room (a couple of centimetres all around is plenty), then lay it in place for a day or two before you fix it in position according to the manufacturer's instructions.

inexpensive coir matting. Close fitted, this has just the right country feel and also makes an excellent background for rugs which, even if not priceless, can at least give an oriental impression. Velvet pile carpet in a plain colour, never patterned, is also a suitable floor covering, but if this is your choice, leave it exposed or add a flat-woven rug like a kelim, since one pile surface somehow looks wrong laid on top of another. Areas of heavy wear like kitchens and halls should have suitably durable surfaces such as flagstones or bricks, but if your budget doesn't run to these undeniably expensive materials, settle for a timber or cork floor, or even vinyl tiles in a plain, unassuming colour or a traditional chequerboard motif – *not* a fake stone or brick pattern.

Fabrics – usually old and faded – are cotton, linen or wool, rather than the much grander brocade or silk. The printed and glazed cotton known as chintz has been the quintessential country-house fabric since the seventeenth century, when the original hand-printed version had to be imported from India; later, of course, it was widely produced in English mills. Intricate examples of needlework, toiled over to pass long winter evenings in the absence of city diversions, are much in evidence.

Windows, like rooms, are large, but since they usually frame spectacular views, overly fussy treatments of any kind are to be avoided. It's important, however, that curtains look full and generous, so if money is tight, splurge

• To tone down bright new textiles (cotton or linen ones only, never delicate fabrics or synthetics), soak them in a solution of household bleach. Begin with a weak solution (about half an egg cupful per litre), then add more very gradually until you get the effect you want. Be sure to rinse the material well in several changes of clean water, or you risk damaging the fibres. Dip pale, plain colours and whites (including those that have gone grey), into an equally weak solution of cold tea or coffee to get an attractively aged effect.

LEFT This formal, yet warm and inviting room owes its mellow charm to the soft glow of the panelling, the imposing portraits, the muted colours, and an eclectic assortment of textiles, furnishings and accessories with the unmistakable patina of age and quality. The windows, although large, are deeply set, so to admit as much light as possible, the pelmet has been positioned above the frame, and the curtains have been fitted with thick rope and tassel tie-backs.

19

- Use cushions and throws to change the look of your room from season to season. In the summer, cover sofas and chairs with light silky shawls, and cushions with pale cotton covers; when winter comes, exchange these for woollen throws in tartan or paisley, and add dark tapestry or needlepoint cushions.

- Salvage the sound portions of a pretty, but worn, rug or carpet to make exotic cushion covers. A domestic sewing machine with a heavyweight needle will cope with light weaves, but for heavy rugs, you'll have to fall back on a pair of stout scissors, an upholsterer's half-circle needle, a reel of heavy thread and a strong pair of hands. Make sure the seams lie flat by trimming them well back and cutting across their corners.

- Age brand-new white or cream lampshades by brushing them with matching emulsion paint, thinned to the consistency of milk; any streaks and blotches will only add to the effect.

on huge quantities of cheap fabric instead of skimping on an expensive one. Apart from their visual appeal, country-house curtains have to keep out draughts, so they contain a layer of thick interlining, giving them an almost padded appearance; to increase their insulating properties, make them long enough to fall on the floor in soft bunches.

Since comfort is of primary importance, every room has plenty of capacious, over-stuffed seating covered with cracked, faded leather, or printed fabric – not in the form of tight upholstery, but as loose covers with a pleated or straight valance. As a finishing touch, drape throws, rugs and shawls over the backs of sofas and chairs, and pile on non-matching cushions decorated with embroidery or tapestry, or made from fabric remnants or fragments of carpet.

Avoid harsh, flattening light by banishing ceiling fittings altogether in favour of king-sized table lamps with plain bases and white or parchment-coloured shades. Few accessories give a more potent country atmosphere than flowers, so have as many around as you can afford, in the form of big, informally mixed bunches in traditional glass or ceramic vases, or as pot-pourri, heaped in huge

bowls and baskets. Finally, Wellington boots and walking sticks left lying near the main entrance will make the most jaded city slicker feel surrounded by rolling hills, as will that most indispensable of all country-house accessories – a large friendly dog.

APPLYING THE STYLE

If the living room, warm and welcoming, is the activity centre of a typical English country house, then its large open fire, irreplaceable for warming hands and toasting teatime crumpets, constitutes the emotional heart. In front of the grate sits a high, leather-upholstered fender, and beside it an enormous basket of logs cut on the estate. A city or suburban fireplace will not be so imposing, but it can still have a nice old fender, and even if the fire is more to do with log-effects than real logs, a roomy basket will be useful for household clutter such as newspapers and toys. Bookshelves are an important feature of the room, and should run from floor to ceiling all along a wall, or in one or more alcoves; to prevent the construction from appearing inappropriately flimsy, use thick,

ABOVE A stout walking stick and a pair of wellies are just as useful for city strolls as country constitutionals. To create the atmosphere of a grand manor house, line them up in the hall with selected items of sporting paraphernalia and a collection of hunting prints.

FAR LEFT Adapt the essential elements of country-house style to suit your own home. Here, coir matting, mixed patterns, generously proportioned furniture, and exotic objects from all over the world give a deceptively pastoral look to a London townhouse.

● Give a wooden picture frame the patina of age by roughing up its surface with a wire brush, going over it with wire wool or sandpaper, then rubbing in a little potting compost, slightly moistened with tinted furniture polish. For the mount, marbled paper will give a softer effect than white or cream card.

stout-looking timber, or add a deep edging for a similar effect. Piles of battered, often-read volumes are bound to spill over on to the floor and nearby tables, so provide plenty of generous surfaces, which will also accommodate sporting magazines and trophies, decoy ducks, stuffed game-birds and fish, family photographs, drinks, and an assortment of card and board games to amuse weekend house guests – complicated jigsaws are particularly popular. A few large pictures are essential, and these should be family portraits – real or make-believe – and country scenes involving as many horses and dogs as possible. Try to add a few exotic-looking accessories – crafted from Indian brass or oriental pottery, perhaps – that suggest a spell of colonial service abroad, or an extended Grand Tour.

In contrast to the living room, a large country-house kitchen eschews comfort and surface prettiness altogether in favour of practicality – originally, of course, only servants used this room, and little effort would have been made on their behalf. As a result, however, the room has a singularly straightforward, no-nonsense appeal, with its massive furniture and natural surfaces of timber, stone and marble. Kitchen life revolves around a huge cast-iron range; these originally burned only solid fuel, but modern ones are suitable for gas, oil and electricity as well. Washing should be done in a deep white porcelain sink fitted with chrome or brass

RIGHT With its plain cream walls, massive freestanding furniture, natural materials and workmanlike equipment, this cavernous country kitchen embodies all the archetypal elements of the style, yet it's just as efficient to work in as a modern fitted one. Old-fashioned rise-and-fall clothes dryers like the one in the corner are still being manufactured, and they're extremely practical even for those with tiny kitchens, since they utilize otherwise dead space.

pillar taps, while a vast, sturdy wooden table provides ample space for preparing food. Strictly speaking, fitted units are inappropriate, so set out glass and china (in a suitable flowery pattern) on a capacious dresser, either freestanding or built in, which can also hold a collection of decorative butter, cheese or jelly moulds; store catering-sized copper saucepans and utensils here too, or suspend them by butcher's hooks from a long metal or wooden rail over the main work area. In the absence of an old-fashioned walk-in larder, display storage jars and attractively packaged foodstuffs on open shelves in a cool corner of the room. These shelves should be fairly shallow so their contents can be easily identified; build them yourself, or try to find an old bookcase that would serve the same purpose. To cope with drips and sticky rings, line the shelves with PVC-covered cotton that extends a little way over the edge to give an attractive finish.

Upstairs, apply the uncontrived, yet elegant, decorating style of the main reception room to the bedrooms, but this time with a slightly lighter touch; the jumble of patterns and objects is similar, but water-colours and flower prints replace the ponderous family portraits, and there are fewer books and trophies scattered around. The main item of furnishing, naturally,

RIGHT There's no need for all your china to match – you'll get a more authentic look by mixing different patterns, as long as these have traditional shapes and a unifying theme such as flowers. Display your nicest plates, jugs, jars and bowls on a huge old dresser like this one, which also has a row of drawers for cutlery and napkins.

is the high, wide bed made from carved wood or polished brass – it may even be a grand four-poster with a large canopy and elaborate drapes. The bed-linen should be pristine white, never patterned, and made from pure linen for preference; blankets used with an eiderdown would be authentic, but a duvet is much lighter and easier to look after, and will give the same effect. Store your clothes in a mammoth old wardrobe and chest of drawers, both of which – curiously – are often cheaper and easier to find than smaller ones, since few homes can accommodate furniture built on the manor-house scale. For a really authentic touch, add a marble-topped wash-stand plus a ewer and basin, or plumb in a small working model.

ABOVE A carved or turned wooden bed made up with fresh white linen and a plump quilt is absolutely typical of a country-house bedroom. Flowery wallpaper, an oriental carpet and plain curtains add to the strong feeling of comfort and prettiness. Note the barley-sugar twist lamp bases that echo the shape of the bedposts.

In contrast to the kitchen, a country-house bathroom is a place for relaxing and feeling pampered. Probably converted from one of the smaller bedrooms, it will have room for a large roll-top bath with claw feet, perhaps positioned in the middle of the room. Like all the sanitary fittings, this should be white – absolutely *never* avocado or pampas – and unadorned, or painted with a traditional design. Walls can be plain, or papered in a pattern similar to those used elsewhere, but on a rather smaller scale; prints and pictures add a homely touch, but if the room is damp, hang a collection of pretty plates instead. Give windows, too, the same kind of treatment as those in the bedroom and living room, or choose classic roller blinds in a pale solid colour or traditional dark green. A separate washstand with an inset basin would be ideal, either an original one or a converted junk-shop sideboard or chest. If you're stuck with an existing pedestal design, attach a gathered skirt (Velcro works well) to soften its lines and provide a useful hidden storage space. Taps should be made of brass with white porcelain trim – x-head fittings for the basin and a telephone-cradle-type mixer for the bath. Hang an assortment of white towels – fine linen hand towels as well as huge fluffy ones – on wall-fixed lengths of brass or chrome, or from a freestanding mahogany towel rail. To complete the effect, provide a small table within easy reach of the bath for a gripping novel and a cool drink.

- Bathroom wallpaper should be made from scrubbable (or at least washable) vinyl, but because this is impervious it can encourage mould, so choose a paste that contains a fungicide or mould inhibitor. If the room is not too damp, you could get away with ordinary paper protected by a proprietary sealant or two coats of matt polyurethane varnish. Do not use either of these on silk or grass papers, however, and always test a small area to make sure the solution won't affect any of the colours.

LEFT Rescued from a second-hand furniture warehouse complete with shower surround and rods, and dinner-plate shower head, this roll-top bath sits happily among extravagant furnishings that make few concessions to the room's practical function. The softly faded curtain fabric is actually a brand new one that's been dipped in cold tea.

English Country Cottage

*T*he furnishing style of a country cottage, like that of a manor house, is appealingly unselfconscious; even though they are both heavily influenced by the exigencies of a life dominated by the land, the cottage look is much simpler, fresher, and more natural, with everything in it designed to suit the modest size of the rooms and their owners' comparatively limited resources. Nothing is grand or sophisticated, and very few items are new, yet the atmosphere is an irresistibly snug and inviting one.

SETTING THE SCENE

Often made from stone, either left uncovered or plastered over, the walls of an old cottage are likely to have rough, undulating surfaces that meet at the corners without forming even remotely square angles. Whatever building material has been used, the traditional finish is whitewash: stone is never left exposed. Whitewash is not actually pure white, so don't assume white paint will give the required effect – go for ivory or buttermilk instead, which are more flattering to most rooms and

furnishings anyway. If, like many cottages, your home tends to be dark, choose a warmer colour still, such as pale blush pink or soft banana yellow. Boldly patterned wallpaper looks wrong, but bedrooms and bathrooms can take delicate, subtly coloured designs printed on a white or pale ground. Strictly speaking, beams should be taken back to their natural colour or painted to match the walls, not picked out in black, which is often too heavy and dominating.

Cottage floors are most usually made from timber, and we have now come to associate a stripped and waxed finish irrevocably with this style. Originally, however, virtually all the wood in poor country houses was painted in soft milky shades – often in a very slap-dash manner – not just for decoration, but to keep out woodworm at a time when proprietary chemicals had yet to be invented. Don't be a slave to authenticity though; if you have beautiful

RIGHT To set off the warm glow of wooden beams and furniture, choose a soft, flattering treatment for your walls like this pale apricot wash.

• To give plastered walls a crude, natural look, use a rectangular block of wood cut across the grain, making sure to blunt the corners slightly; at all costs, avoid fake combed or swirled textures. If you're simply repainting, wait until the last coat of emulsion is dry, then go over it lightly with fine sandpaper to highlight small irregularities. Avoid the joins on paper-lined walls, though, since any slight abrasion will make them more obvious.

• To make diminutive cottage-style rooms look larger, paint the skirting boards to match the floor rather than picking them out in white, or blending them in with the walls.

RIGHT Many cottages have brick or stone floors, softened with rugs and carpets. In this comfortably cluttered passage between kitchen and dining room, all the furniture has been given a natural wax finish or a coat of eggshell paint.

hardwood floors, leave them alone or add a coat of wax – not shiny varnish; inexpensive softwood floorboards, on the other hand, might benefit from the traditional painted treatment. Floors, like walls, were seldom flat and even, so a typical cottage room contains three-legged tables and stools, which are reasonably stable on a bumpy surface.

Costly, polished woods like mahogany are not suitable for cottage furniture, which is usually made from something cheaper such as pine. Here too, a painted finish is most correct, but a stripped and waxed one has a charm that is hard to resist. Remember though, that natural wood furniture bought new will almost certainly have a coat of protective lacquer, and can therefore never acquire the glowing patina that comes from layers of beeswax affectionately rubbed in. Cupboard, drawer and door handles should be made from brass or undecorated white porcelain.

Cottage fabrics are natural, even homespun-looking, in soft, solid colours or uncomplicated patterns (ordinary mattress ticking has an appropriately unpretentious quality) and left unadorned by fringe, tassels and braid. Because windows

BELOW For most country dwellers, keeping out the cold is a major priority; in this grander-than-average cottage, solid oak panelling and thick curtains provide a high degree of insulation.

are small – and often deep as well – light is precious, so hang short, neat curtains from a plain brass, iron or wooden rail (never plastic track) that extends far enough beyond the edges of the window for the fabric to be pulled completely clear. For a charming effect, make your curtains from hand-woven Indian cotton in white or cream, then add a delicately embroidered motif at the bottom corners, or along the leading edges and the hem.

To get the lighting right, invest in several table lamps that aren't too fussy, or look for oil ones that have been converted to electricity; one or two left in their original state will give a characteristically soft, gentle illumination.

Most accessories – rugs and baskets, for example – serve a useful function, and although many are beautifully hand-made, there is an absence of purely decorative crafts such as very intricate embroidery or *petit point*, which are too time-consuming to be justified. One item of domestic needlework that no cottage should be without, however, is a quilt – or preferably several – since their use is by no means restricted to the bedroom: fold a favourite specimen over the back of the sofa, for instance, to provide warmth on chilly evenings; hang one at the window to keep out draughts and replace conventional curtains; or drape one over an ugly table. If you can find an old quilt being sold cheaply in a junk shop or flea market because it's worn or stained, buy it and cut it up to make charming

- If the view from your windows is less than green and pleasant, give the effect of outside foliage by fixing shelves across them to hold rows of trailing plants; be sure to make these shelves removable for cleaning. Alternatively, hang pots from the reveal, or stand them on tiny shelves fixed to it securely.

LEFT Applied with care and sensitivity, some interior design styles can give a new lease of life to buildings that may have outlived their original purpose. This stable block retains a number of its characteristic features – and all of its charm – in a conversion that makes the most of the cottagey look, with daintily patterned curtains, a coat of fresh white paint, and a collection of country furniture, antique curios and homely accessories.

- Invented in the United States at the end of the nineteenth century, Lloyd Loom furniture is made from spun kraft paper woven with paper-wrapped wire. It has the same rustic look as cane, is just as strong and light, and can be moulded into similar curvy shapes, yet it doesn't split or crack and is even immune to attack from woodworm. After being out of production for many years, Lloyd Loom chairs and tables are once again being made to the original designs, and although these are just as handsome as the originals, they are no longer as cheap. If you're lucky, you may find some old pieces in a second-hand shop; a coat of car spray paint will give them a new lease of life.

- To keep a hardwood work surface looking its best, use sandpaper or wire wool to get rid of small marks or stains, then treat it with an oil recommended for that particular timber; be sure to rub off any excess, or it could go rancid. Raise small dents with a damp rag and a warm iron, but go carefully, since you risk scorching the wood if the iron's too hot.

cushions. One of the nicest ways to display a much-loved quilt is by hanging it on the wall like a tapestry; most are pretty enough to be shown off in this way, even though English quilting is usually done on white or a single printed fabric with a plain or striped backing, rather than on the multi-coloured patchwork favoured by Americans.

Probably the most typical decorative element in a cottage is country-garden flowers like daisies, cow parsley, delphiniums, lupins or even rose-hips, stuffed casually into jugs and bowls, never arranged in stiff formal shapes. When winter comes, use leaves and boughs instead, and display dried flowers in pretty baskets, or hung in generous bunches from the ceiling.

APPLYING THE STYLE

In common with country-house living rooms, those in cottages are arranged around a fire, but here the surround and basket are smaller and less ornate, and the accessories are roughly fashioned, with no fancy embellishments or gilding. The few homely sofas and chairs have loose covers whose generous fit and gathered valance give an almost baggy effect; plump feather seat and back cushions look nicer than unyielding foam ones. Provide occasional seating in the form of a cane or Lloyd Loom chair, or one in a traditional Windsor design, which might be improved by a fresh coat of paint to disguise darkened varnish. Ladder-back chairs with rush seats

are archetypal cottage items, and a collection of these, whether they match or not, will do double duty around the table at meal times – an old church pew is also useful here, or in a kitchen or hall. The thickness of cottage walls often allows enough depth under a window to install a window seat which, with the addition of cushions, makes a pleasant bolt-hole.

A large, sturdy pine table will cater for a multitude of activities in addition to dining, as will a traditional oak gate-leg model with barley-sugar-twist legs. Again, paint over darkened varnish, or strip it off and add a wax finish. A coffee table, although not an authentically rustic item, is too useful to do without, so press into service a wooden chest or blanket box, which can double up as storage or even as additional guest seating.

At the cosy heart of a country cottage is its kitchen, and this often acts as a kind of informal sitting room too, with rugs on the floor and a comfy chair or sofa near the stove; because the family spends so much time here, no effort is spared to make it attractive and welcoming. Tongue and groove cladding, perhaps to dado height, looks lovely, especially when given a coat of paint in a fresh, subtle colour with a silk or eggshell finish. Naturally there are no fitted units, but if you don't yearn enough for pastoral charm to give them up, look for a range in natural or painted wood that has no extraneous ornamentation or detailing. Many such ranges

include decor panels that neatly camouflage unlovely modern appliances like washing machines and tumble driers. You might be able to get the best of both worlds by searching out several freestanding furnishing items – a chest of drawers, perhaps, or an old wardrobe, painted and fitted out with shelves – then installing a hardwood work surface with a plain white tiled splashback along one wall. Conceal the storage space underneath with a gathered skirt that can be removed for washing.

The pretty dresser is smaller

RIGHT As well as supplying cooking facilities and general warmth, the traditional cast-iron range acts as an efficient dryer for tea towels, clothing and, occasionally, flowers.

● Old bits of china are still fairly easy to find at junk shops, flea markets and car boot sales, but they're often stained or discoloured. To improve their appearance, soak them in a solution of household bleach, denture cleaner or biological washing powder. Don't be tempted to use these tactics on painted tinware, however, or you could dissolve the decoration entirely.

RIGHT In this cosy, informal bedroom, virtually every surface is strewn with pretty pink roses, from tight buds to full-blown blooms. If freehand furniture painting is beyond your scope, use stencils or even paper cut-outs, varnished for protection.

than its country-house relation, but its function is the same – to house a collection of china. Here, though, you're likely to find natural pottery or glazed white earthenware, left plain or adorned with a tiny, delicate pattern rather than an overblown flowery one. Also set out on these shelves are rows of jars containing bottled fruit and vegetables, home-made preserves and pickles, and similar evidence of thrifty housekeeping. Provide additional storage capacity by installing a plate rack over the sink and fixing a hanging rail for saucepans (cast iron or enamel rather than copper), herbs and strings of onions. Similarly, keep your eggs in an open wicker basket, and your fruit and vegetables on display in hand-made trugs.

In the centre of the room, a large wooden table with a drawer at one end and a well-scrubbed surface serves as the main food preparation area; at meal times, a cheerful checked cloth, soft and faded from repeated washing, is laid on top.

A real cottage bedroom is often tucked up under the eaves, resulting in its characteristically small size and pitched ceiling, so this style is particularly suitable for box rooms, or those carved out of a loft or attic conversion. To minimize awkward angles and corners, cover both walls and ceiling with small-print wallpaper, or at least paint them the same colour. Choose an old-fashioned bed made from brass, painted wrought iron or wood; even an ordinary divan will do, if you hang some-

- Add a charming finish to white bed-linen by stitching narrow cotton lace along the top edge of flat sheets and the open end of pillowcases. Or choose delicate satin ribbon in white or a pale pastel colour to tie in with the rest of the room.

thing pretty like a decorative mirror or a cot quilt at its head. Bedding should be made from spotless white cotton: a silky or frilly coverlet looks wrong, so go for an unsophisticated design in white or cream, plain or crocheted, or – the obvious choice – another quilt. Snowy *broderie anglaise* would make ideal cushions or curtains. Store clothes in a modestly designed and proportioned wardrobe and chest of drawers, and provide extra storage capacity in the form of a large hamper or chest – in wicker, wood or painted tin – that can also double as a bedside table. To add a finishing touch, fasten a sprig of fragrant herbs like thyme, rosemary or bay to your bedhead with a length of dainty ribbon.

FAR LEFT This tiny, potentially awkward room has been cleverly pulled together with a pale, small-print wallpaper that extends uninterrupted over the ceiling. The same pattern has been chosen for the curtains, cushions and coverlet, thus providing subtle relief from an otherwise all-white scheme that prevents the room from feeling claustrophobic.

LEFT Fresh, delicate white flowers in a simple vase will add a pastoral touch to any room. Here, an inexpensive bamboo table sits beside the bath to provide a surface for toiletries, plus a shelf underneath for towels.

In the bathroom, consider once again installing tongue and groove cladding up to dado height; bring it out from the wall slightly to conceal the plumbing and add a narrow shelf along the top to provide a useful place for toiletries. The floor should have a natural finish (if not timber, then matt-sealed cork tiles) with a flat cotton rug on top, not a shaggy towelling one shaped to fit around the basin or toilet. Look for a range of wooden accessories (shelf, towel rail etc), then add a small chair for towels, and perhaps a little table to hold a jug of flowers; bottles and jars can be stored in open baskets or on the shelves of a layered plant stand. If space is tight, suspend a drawstring laundry bag from the back of the door.

French Provençal

While they have many things in common with rural dwellings all over the world, Provençal houses have an individual style that is deeply linked to the soothing warmth and abundant sunshine that are such a feature of life in the south of France. Their cool rooms are sparsely furnished and uncontrived, and everything in them seems to have been chosen because it is greatly cherished or perfectly suited for a practical purpose. Much of the day is spent outdoors, and the surrounding garden is almost an extension of the house; inside, pungent smells fill every room, the sweet scent of herbs and flowers mixing with the seductive aromas of fresh coffee, simmering soups and newly baked bread.

SETTING THE SCENE
Primarily designed to keep out the summer sun, Provençal rooms have low ceilings and thick walls unevenly washed with a warm colour like dairy cream, light gold, peachy pink, or a pale version of the quintessential colour of Provence – terracotta. To get a similarly luminous effect in more northern climes, go for more intense (but still subtle) versions of these hues, such as dusty rose, tawny apricot or a rich honey shade; lavender blue and deep violet are typical colours too, but they could give a distinctly chilly cast in less intense sunlight. Skirtings and mouldings should be coloured and finished to match the walls (no gloss paint, though), a treatment that is flattering to all small rooms and to those with odd shapes or irregular detailing.

Although timber, stone and brick are used fairly widely, the most traditional – and the most common – floor covering for every room is locally fired terracotta tiles. Small rugs are laid on top in colours selected to blend with the tiles rather than add contrast.

There is very little built-in furniture, but typical pieces are massive and beautifully crafted; unpretentious yet graceful, these are usually made from walnut or fruit-wood and decorated with

---

RIGHT Add a touch of Provence to a sunny corner by filling it with bright blooms in hand-painted pots.
Matching tiles transform a plain table.

- To imitate the faded, uneven effect of colour-washing, begin by applying a coat of emulsion paint in the usual way. Then, when it's dry, give a feeling of depth by adding another coat in a slightly darker or lighter shade of the same colour, thinned down with water. Use a large brush, and make long, wide, irregular strokes in different directions to achieve a patchy, but appealingly translucent, surface that looks authentic, yet is easy to clean. If your room is newly plastered, don't paint it at all – just apply a matt sealer like ship's varnish.

- Concrete floors can be colour-washed (see above) to give the effect of terracotta, or just painted using a suitable rusty shade. If you want a warmer surface underfoot, lay vinyl tiles in a similar plain colour, but avoid those that try to imitate the look of terracotta or quarry tiles.

- Loose rugs laid on top of a hard floor can easily slip and cause a nasty accident, especially if your household includes children or elderly people. To be safe, anchor all rugs and small carpets with purpose-made webbing or underlay.

hand carving or naïvely painted images that have faded from exposure to the sun.

Adding bright splashes of colour all over the house are the distinctive Provençal fabrics with their small, intensely coloured motifs: this material has been produced in Tarascon by the same family (the Demérys) for over 200 years, and was originally inspired by seventeenth-century hand-painted Indian textiles. Today it is still widely used for upholstery, cushions, quilts, tablecloths and the unlined curtains that hang from a simple rail at each window. Crunchy cotton lace is also popular for this purpose, but whatever fabric you choose, keep it clear of the glass with an archetypal French accessory, a hook-shaped tie-back made from brass and fixed to the frame. An alternative window treatment is stained wooden shutters, which not only shut out the sun, but also offer protection from the cold and unpredictable mistral.

Another absolutely essential ingredient is flowers – display blooms that abound in Provence such as lilac, hydrangea, campanula, wisteria and geraniums in pretty jugs, or fill dark, hand-made wicker baskets and huge terracotta pots with massed bunches of the fragrant lavender that is one of the region's main exports.

APPLYING THE STYLE

In many Provençal homes, the living room is for special occasions and important visitors only – the family spend most of their time

- If your sewing skills are minimal, buy cotton lace in a panel rather than by the metre; choose a size that is at least 1½ times as wide as your window (or two panels to make up this width), and the same length, or slightly longer. Then, simply stitch curtain heading tape along the top, and slip in the hooks. If your panel is too long, measure the excess and position the tape this distance from the top; when your curtain is hung, the end will fold over to make a pretty pelmet. For extra-large windows, use a lace tablecloth or even a bedspread instead of a window panel.

LEFT A capacious armoire will take care of endless household clutter while giving an authentically French look. In this stylish sitting room, small windows, a cool brick floor and crisp white fabrics help to counteract the hot summer sun.

either outdoors or in the kitchen. There will be a large curly fire-place, though, and a king-sized sofa with deep, voluminous cushions. Occasional seating is provided by painted cane or wicker chairs, also comfortably padded, that can be shifted easily when the action moves into the garden.

Since eating plays a major part in the life of a French household, the kitchen is unquestionably its emotional hub, a meeting place for family members and friends as well as an efficient centre for the preparation of meals, and an inviting setting for their unhurried consumption – fast food has no place in this way of life. A chequerboard floor in black (or terracotta) and white tiles is absolutely typical, and work surfaces, too, are often made from plain ceramic tiles. Dominating the room are a solid cast-iron range and the ubiquitous large table; if your kitchen is small, a wooden slatted folding table or a marble-topped one – both of which are common in French cafés – will give an authentically Gallic atmosphere and save space. A huge armoire holds bulky equipment, but here, even more than in other country kitchens, food, china and the all-important *batterie de cuisine* are displayed on open shelves. Often charmingly edged with a narrow band of white lace, these reflect the philosophy that anything well-made and suited to its purpose is also beautiful. Implements are basic rather than tricksy; while there should be an excellent collection of sharp

LEFT Use a bright yellow scheme to simulate Mediterranean sunlight, then reinforce the effect with jumbo chequerboard floor tiles, rustic terracotta pots, and sturdy wooden furniture. Here, a lightweight chair is poised by the door, ready to provide outdoor seating. Nothing in this potentially ordinary kitchen is costly, since all the furniture was bought second-hand – the cheerful and welcoming effect has been achieved solely by using colour and paint imaginatively, and by having the courage to keep everything else simple and uncluttered.

carbon-steel knives, an egg slicer has no place here. If you are reluctant to adopt this exposed idiom wholeheartedly, install glass-fronted cupboards instead of those with solid doors as a working compromise. Whether they're on shelves or tucked away in cupboards, dry goods should be kept in classic pot-bellied glass preserving jars, wooden bins or crocks made from the local salt-glazed stoneware; this distinctive pearly pottery is also used to make vessels for slow-cooking dishes like cassoulets and terrines. The special tin-glazed earthenware called *faïence* is made in this region, and its thick rustic design, warm ochre colour and charmingly primitive decoration would be attractive in most kitchens. If you prefer something simpler, look for the similarly chunky white china that has a pretty edge and a hint of natural clay colour grinning through its glaze. Rough wine in sturdy tumblers is drunk at most meals, which are served – naturally – on a bright Provençal cloth; to avoid constant washing, choose a design that is available in PVC-covered cotton, which is easy to wipe clean after use.

RIGHT A roomy freestanding cupboard like this one, with its deep marble shelf, fitted baskets and built-in wine-racks, can act as a mini-larder in all but the smallest city kitchen. Inside is a distinctly Gallic collection of bottled fruit and vegetables, whole cheeses, dried (and drying) herbs, fresh bread, and a wide range of pungent comestibles.

French bedrooms are frequently spare chambers with very little furniture or decoration, yet their atmosphere is private and calming rather than uncomfortable or ascetic. The floor is likely to be timber, which is not painted, but left in its natural state or treated with a translucent stain. The most important feature in the room is the bed, which is usually positioned along a wall rather than projecting into the room. If the frame is made from brass or iron, it will probably be rather curvier than its English counterpart; many Provençal beds, however, are made from wood, elaborately

ABOVE The almost monastic look of this bedroom has been softened and sophisticated by replacing traditional white bedlinen with a co-ordinated range in a riotously flowery pattern. On the floor however, locally made tiles anchor the scheme firmly in the French countryside.

carved at the head and with low posts at the foot, or crafted in the traditional *bateau lit* shape that elsewhere is sometimes called a sleigh bed. Here, too, sheets and pillowcases should be white cotton, with a blanket or duvet for warmth and an equally pristine white counterpane on top, or a quilted one made from the indigenous fabric. Large square pillows supported by a long thick bolster are an essential French element, as is another imposing armoire to store clothing and accessories. A small table covered with a crisp white cloth will cope with bedside necessities, and the only wall decoration should be a simple religious artefact such as a cross.

If you are used to bathing in a room that is festooned with pipes, this is the style for you, since exposed plumbing is a feature of many French bathrooms. Despite their somewhat basic appearance, they are efficiently planned, with white fittings that are, like the rest of the furnishings, over-sized and functional. The bath is often in the centre of the room and beside the toilet there is always a bidet. If it weren't for softening touches like a small bouquet of wild flowers or a pretty mirror, the feeling would be almost clinical, since tiles, also in white, often cover the walls up to dado or picture-rail height; to add a typically smart detail, fix a narrow border of dark blue ones. Ceramic tiles would be a good choice for the floor as well; they're expensive, but the area to be covered may be small enough to bring them within your budget.

RIGHT Converted from an existing space, this classic all-white bathroom contains a wide variety of contrasting textures (marble, plaster, lace, linen), plus plenty of natural materials such as brick, wood, cane and brass, that keep it from looking cold and stark. In the corner, a plain table has been covered with several layers of antique lace for an opulent effect. To copy this idea, you need only one really nice cloth, since you can hide damaged or stained ones underneath. Coarse, slubby white fabric filters the light appealingly, so use a pair of old, real linen, hand-towels instead of curtains at a small window, or cut down a single-bed sheet or a tablecloth in the same material to fit a larger one.

American Traditional

The homes in colonial America were naturally heavily influenced by those in the European countries from which the early settlers had come, particularly England and Germany. Later, distinctive American styles were born out of an attractive mix of treasured furnishings transported across the ocean with simple rustic things made locally, using available timbers and a small collection of tools. Some of the most distinctive elements such as patchwork and stencilling were the result of having to improvise and make do with the limited materials to hand.

EASTERN STYLE

The north-eastern corner of the United States was the first area to be widely populated, and the pretty wooden houses in late-eighteenth-century New England and New York were exceptionally elegant and comfortable. Walls were painted or washed in soft cream or off-white, with all the woodwork – doors and door frames, window frames, skirting board and even shelves – picked out in a deeper shade; today, this detailing should be done in a silk or eggshell finish that resembles the subtle sheen of old pigment. A common feature was tongue and groove cladding (matchboarding) fixed up to dado-rail (chair-rail) height, and painted to match the woodwork. All the colours used in the decoration of colonial rooms would have come from vegetable pigments, with the result that they were rich and intense, and yet extremely subtle; look for bayberry (a muted grey-green), blue-tinged forest green, mustard yellow, cranberry, nutmeg brown, or the dark red known as turkey red (or sometimes barn red, from the finish commonly applied to farm buildings).

Floors were made from a hardwood like maple and polished to give a deep, golden glow; you could get a similar effect with parquet tiles treated in the same way. On top of this, there would have been a collection of rugs:

RIGHT No item of furniture is more strongly associated with colonial America than the rocking chair, which many people believe was invented by the statesman Benjamin Franklin.

- A real hardwood floor is not only beautiful to look at, but also extremely durable and warm underfoot – and it complements a huge range of furnishing styles as well. DIY enthusiasts can lay the boards themselves, with expert advice; you can buy them ready sealed, but for a deep, rich patina, apply several layers of wax yourself, polishing each one well before you add the next.

- With the availability of modern materials, floor-cloths are easier to make, and harder-wearing, than they were in their heyday. There are several excellent reference books that explain the technique, which basically involves applying primer, paint and varnish on to a sheet of canvas. Experiment first on a small mat, perhaps for a child's room or hallway, that you can work on at the convenient height of your kitchen table.

RIGHT A twentieth-century house meticulously decorated in late eighteenth-century style, Hidden Glen near Philadelphia embodies many of the period's typical features: plain walls with contrast detailing, a polished timber floor, primitive portraits and accent colours of blue-green and turkey red.

hand-made hooked, braided or rag rugs in ordinary households, and flower-strewn needlepoint ones for the more affluent. Another common accessory was a painted floor-cloth, the inexpensive fore-runner of linoleum and carpet.

Furniture, too, was crafted from highly polished wood, and typical items were corner cupboards, dressers (called hutches), chests of drawers (called dressers) and capacious pieces such as the characteristic blanket chest with a lidded upper section and one or more drawers in the base. Beds were commonly made from wood as well, and often resembled a restrained version of the traditional four-poster, sometimes with a truckle, or trundle, bed (a low bed on wheels) underneath. (The cabinet-makers and craftsmen who made these large items also produced finely turned wooden kitchen utensils – spoons, ladles, rolling pins and cups – commonly called treenware.)

A sofa in one of these houses would not have differed greatly from a European one, and wing chairs were also common here, as were the Windsor variety; imported from England at first, these were later manufactured in such huge quantities in the United States that they became almost as closely associated with America as with England. One item of occasional seating that is inextricably linked with this style is the wooden rocking chair, which was invented in America in the eighteenth century.

Louvred shutters or wooden

52

• In terms of filling, there are two kinds of quilt: plump ones stuffed with feathers, which are usually machine-quilted in large geometric shapes; and thinner ones filled with layers of cloth, which are hand quilted in complex swirling patterns. The best way to clean both types is by putting them in an automatic washing machine set to a short, cool programme; lifting a wet, enormously heavy, quilt while hand washing it is likely to stretch it out of shape permanently. Feather quilts should be dried naturally, but cloth-filled ones are better off in a cool tumble drier. However, if your quilt is old and fragile, take it to a specialist cleaners.

• The huge range of products on the market makes it possible for you to decorate your home quickly, easily and cheaply using stencilled motifs. Look for a ready-cut stencil (those made from clear acetate allow you to see the whole design at once), or cut one yourself, based on or matching the pattern on a favourite fabric or wallpaper. When it comes to colours, you'll get the right subtle effect with either car spray paints or crayon-like sticks of solid colour, which are by far the easiest to use.

venetian blinds were used at windows, as were crisp café curtains, gathered and hung from a simple metal or wooden pole fixed halfway up the frame to afford privacy without cutting out all the light; combine these with louvred shutters to give another authentic look.

Softening benches and settles as well as adorning beds were characteristically colourful quilts often made from sound portions of old clothing and soft furnishings cut out and sewn together in one of the many patchwork patterns, or appliquéd on to a fabric backing. Other textiles – rough homespun, neat gingham checks and tiny calico prints – were plainer, and quilt-less beds would be draped with a white candlewick coverlet.

The other craft that is strongly associated with the American look is stencilling: this was originally devised to imitate printed wallpapers and fabrics, which were very expensive and difficult to obtain. (Later, ironically, papers and fabrics were designed to look like hand stencilling.) Cut into stylized flower, fruit and animal shapes, stencils were used to decorate not only walls, but also furniture, floors (where they were meant to look like area rugs), and window blinds. Stencilled motifs could be

used to cover a whole area or to add a neat border at cornice level or around a window. People either did the stencilling themselves or hired an itinerant painter, called a limner, to do it for them; these journeyman artists also covered walls with huge murals depicting rural scenes, historical tableaux and Bible stories, and went in for a little gentle portrait painting on the side.

To give a colonial feel to your rooms, try to find a few authentic-looking accessories like a needlework sampler; a primitive portrait or landscape; a decoy duck; a slender curving metal chandelier; or a bird or animal-shaped weather vane. Any object shaped like, or adorned with, a pineapple would add the perfect touch, since pineapples were a symbol of hospitality in early American homes.

ABOVE In one of Hidden Glen's bedrooms, the characteristically simple scheme focuses attention on a pair of quilts appliquéd with bold red-and-green flowers.

FAR LEFT Bright red stencil motifs with a Pennsylvania Dutch flavour decorate every part of this cheerful little attic bedroom – the floor, the walls, the window and even the bed.

Pennsylvania Dutch

In Pennsylvania, slightly to the south of New York and New England, lived a community of German immigrants ('Dutch' in this context is a corruption of deutsch, or German) who decorated their homes and their furniture using the bright exuberant colours and forms so popular in the alpine areas of their own country. Kitchen implements as well as wardrobes and chests were painted with simple, stylized fruits, flowers, birds and animals, often facing each other in pairs; sometimes the shapes were even cut out of flat surfaces such as chair backs. Tinware painted with these brilliant motifs is another typically Pennsylvania Dutch craft – you could substitute the reasonably similar oriental cups, bowls and plates.

Shaker

In retrospect, the American vernacular style that has had perhaps the most lasting design influence, both in the USA and abroad, is that of a small religious sect that fled from England in the mid-1700s – the Shakers. Dedicated to the belief that order, simplicity and good craftsmanship should govern the look of things, they insisted that rooms were open and spare, with clear surfaces and a complete lack of adornment of any kind. These austere yet breathtakingly elegant rooms contained very little, but they were nevertheless supremely practical, and the furniture in them was designed with such purity of line and pleasing proportions that nearly 200 years later there is still a

RIGHT Although the severe Shaker way of life has all but died out completely, their stunningly simple and beautiful rooms are increasingly valued by those who have no time for gimmicky, overblown decorative effects. This typical bedroom or 'retiring room' is arranged in dormitory fashion to sleep four or five people in narrow single beds – since they believed firmly in chastity, the Shakers never made double ones. The homespun checked cloth provided insulation on the same principle as a medieval tapestry, and the soapstone slab underneath the woodburning stove would have been used to warm the sheets. While each piece of furniture was designed to fulfil a particular function, the famous round and oval boxes were originally produced for sale, to bring in much-needed money for supplies.

ABOVE *The elegant ladderback chair is another Shaker classic; in this spartan dining room, a matching set has been arranged around a sturdy table laid with plain white china. Note how the shelves in the purpose-built cupboard have been spaced to accommodate items of different sizes.*

large international market for reproduction Shaker chairs, chests, benches and small round-topped candle stands. Every item was designed to fit its space and its purpose, with each built-in storage unit specifically designed for its contents, and precisely labelled so everything could be put back in its place after use. Rooms were decorated like the plainest colonial ones, with cream walls, and woodwork painted the sombre colour sometimes called meeting-house green after the Shakers' place of worship. Running around the walls, just above shoulder height, was a pegboard – a length of timber with short pieces of dowel projecting from it at regular intervals. Almost any item in everyday use could be hung from these pegs, including chairs, small cupboards, articles of clothing, baskets and bags, and candle sconces and cutting boards, thus keeping the floor and table constantly clear and easy to clean; a variation of this ingenious storage system would work well in many modern homes, especially where space is tight. Perhaps the best-known Shaker item is the round or oval storage box; made of steamed wood, each one would be individually stained in dull yellow, orangey red, blue or bottle green to identify its contents. This use of a very small range of colours was one of the few types of decoration accepted by the uncompromising Shaker philosophy.

WESTERN STYLE

The pioneers who travelled across the country to its south-west corner to make their fortunes were faced with a landscape, climate and way of life that were very different from those they had left behind, and their homes expressed this dramatically. Even today these houses look much as they always have, since their style (sometimes known as 'Tex-Mex') reflects the

LEFT Large expanses of bare white plaster, dark, massive furniture and locally hand-made textiles mark the style of the settlers who colonized the American south-west. Reinforcing the strong geometric feeling of this lofty, arched room, a collection of striped rag rugs has been displayed on the table, the sofa and the wall, as well as laid out on the sun-bleached timber floorboards. When the temperature outside is scorching, thick stone walls and firmly bolted wooden shutters keep the interior cool and comfortable.

same main influences: the relentlessly hot temperatures, and the proximity of two very different cultures – those of the native Indians and of Mexico to the south.

To reflect the dazzling sun, the rough stone or plaster walls are painted white. The floors are made of cool stone; oiled concrete would give a similar look. Here, too, there is an absence of decorative detailing or pattern, but the little that exists is bold, brilliantly coloured and often of Mexican or Indian origin. Although one or two pieces of furniture may be finely fashioned, most of it is rough-hewn and sturdy and some items like benches and cupboards are built in; wood is reddish in tinge, or bleached. Typical accessories are bright Navajo rugs with chevron and diamond motifs, hung on walls and draped on tables as well as laid on the floor. Look for druggets or dhurries from India in similarly graphic designs, and search out big bright Spanish pots to imitate the look of those made in Mexico. Instead of leafy plants and flowers, choose a big spiky cactus, or arrange one or two sun-bleached or dried branches in a large earthenware crock or plain glass vase.

To add a witty, Hollywood-western touch that is also extremely practical, replace your kitchen door with saloon-type swing panels that hide the worst of the clutter without cutting off the room entirely. In addition, you will save the space that would otherwise be needed for door clearance.

LEFT Homespun gingham in fresh bright colours is perhaps the fabric we associate most strongly with American pioneer life. Above these cheerful curtains, timber louvres keep out heat and light while admitting as much air as possible; to take advantage of this, bunches of herbs have been hung in front of the window to dry. Near the oven, the cook has assembled the equipment and ingredients necessary to prepare a meal for hungry workers.

Swedish Country

The vernacular Swedish style that has had the longest-lasting international influence is probably that associated with the painter Carl Larsson at the turn of the twentieth century. In an extensive collection of pictures that sold thousands of copies in book form, Larsson lovingly documented every corner and decorative detail of the bright, cheerful country house he and his wife Karin had decorated. Larsson's work was much more than an album of his own home, however; his conscious intention in publishing his paintings was to disseminate his own strongly held views about interior design, which evolved (this was the case with several other furnishing philosophies of the time) as a reaction against the clutter and stuffiness of late-nineteenth-century rooms.

Essentially, the Larsson style involved mixing elegant things with rustic ones, grand rococo furniture from the heyday of Swedish design (the Gustavian period at the end of the eighteenth century), with contemporary pieces and simple country objects, colours and patterns. The most striking feature, though, was the clear fresh colours and bright airiness of his rooms, both reflecting the preoccupation of so many northern cultures with the sunlight they so seldom see.

SETTING THE SCENE

To re-create the Larsson look, wash your walls with off-white or pale grey, and add a painted or stencilled border, at cornice level only, or along the skirting and vertically at the corners as well to form panels: garlands and ribbons are typical motifs. Alternatively, choose that universally popular country treatment, tongue and groove cladding to dado or picture-rail height; if you extend this to the higher level, fix a wide shelf at the top, supported by simple brackets, to display a collection of pretty plates. Wallpaper would not look appropriate in the living room, but a dainty floral stripe is fine for a bedroom.

Floors should be made from wooden boards – painted, or scrubbed and bleached grey by the sun; in this case, parquet tiles won't give the right look. On top of these boards, in most country homes, were very long, narrow runners, hand woven in colourful

---

RIGHT Create the all-important impression of light by choosing pale colours and adding a touch of greenery.

- If your floorboards are in poor condition, use a proprietary floor paint on them instead of trying for a natural look. Before you begin, fill any cracks to give a better surface and prevent draughts: then, once the paint is dry, apply several coats of matt sealant. Any painted finish will fade slightly, becoming softer and prettier with time, but it's a good idea to protect it with a new coat of sealant every year or two.

To give the effect of old, limed wood, strip boards right back, sand them down, then rub a little white emulsion into the bare wood in the direction of the grain, removing any excess paint as you go.

stripes and neatly arranged to form walkways along areas of heavy traffic.

It was not uncommon for windows to be left completely unadorned, but in the main they were hung with roller blinds, or with solid shutters to keep out the wind and cold. A signature element of this style is a touch of filmy white fabric like muslin or calico used to soften the effect, either in the form of a pretty gathered pelmet, or as simple dress curtains, both of which were originally devised to admit the maximum amount of precious light.

APPLYING THE STYLE

The country furniture in Larsson's rooms was homely and even a little crude, while the antiques were slender and light with tapered legs; both types should be strong and practical without looking bulbous or heavy. Wood was left natural, limed to give a bleached effect, or painted – white, grey, pale yellow, blue and brown were popular colours – and frequently decorated with a subtly coloured motif, either stencilled or painted on free-hand. Chairs and sofas had intricately carved frames that, far from being deeply upholstered in the Victorian fashion, were given only a thin layer of padding. This was covered with one of the crisp, fresh-looking materials (such as checked or striped linen in pink or blue) that were used all over the house for things like tablecloths and bed hangings. One curiously characteristic piece of furniture was a

LEFT A floor-to-ceiling wood-burning stove clad entirely in hand-painted tiles (these have a subtle spatter decoration) provides the dominant feature in many Swedish country rooms. Another distinctive element is the pale timber floor with its narrow, hand-woven stripey runners that mark out main traffic paths. Much of the traditional furniture is from the Gustavian period, which takes its name from King Gustav III who ruled towards the end of the eighteenth century. As well as inspiring the apotheosis of Swedish design, this intelligent, enthusiastic and generous patron of the arts was also a well-respected playwright.

LEFT The combination of simple checked fabrics with elegant antique furniture is one of the hallmarks of the Larsson style, as is the limed finish on these delicate pieces.

FAR LEFT Tongue and groove cladding painted with a fresh, bright colour can help to disguise fitted cupboards in an awkwardly shaped bathroom. Here, concealed downlighters add a note of twentieth-century practicality.

wooden rocking chair; during this period, these were being widely imported from the United States, where they had been found and appreciated by the Swedish people who emigrated there in the last century.

One of the most common features in these houses was the enormous solid-fuel stove, which usually extended from floor to ceiling and stood on a zinc platform. This necessarily efficient appliance was sometimes placed in the corner of a room and added greatly to the decorative appeal with its all-over cladding of ceramic tiles, hand painted with flowers, swags or classical urns. If you

have a similar stove, try embellishing it with a *trompe-l'oeil* tiled pattern using special paints that are designed to withstand high temperatures.

In terms of small accessories, look for oil lamps, brass or tin chandeliers and sturdy candlesticks; on the wall, arrange groups of small pictures, perhaps in plain round or oval frames. Add touches of white lace or crochet in the form of table-mats, doilies, traycloths, runners or old-fashioned antimacassars, and try to see that there are always one or two prettily trailing plants and a small bunch of artlessly arranged meadow flowers.

EXOTIC STYLE

❦

*G*ive your rooms a welcome injection of colour and excitement by looking to far-off lands and dramatically different cultures for design inspiration. Without attempting the wholesale re-creation of a style that perhaps has little relevance to your way of life, you can adapt its underlying principles, borrow one or more of its visual characteristics, or combine some of its more accessible elements with what you already have to create your own very distinctive schemes.

Tropical

From the Caribbean to the Mediterranean, searing temperatures, abundant light and the proximity of the sea seem to encourage common design characteristics: the colours are intense, the division between inside and out is blurred, and one of the main priorities is keeping cool.

This is essentially a simple, native style characterized by endless white surfaces set off with splashes of coral pink, sea turquoise, sky blue, sunshine yellow and palm-leaf green. In less sultry climates, enhance rather than discourage warmth by choosing a shade of white that has a hint of pink or yellow in it, or by using lots of warm accent colours rather than the chillier blues and greens that are so popular in hot countries.

In order to take advantage of every light breeze, tropical houses are often open plan, so these ideas would adapt well to modern dwellings with a similar layout.

CREATING THE LOOK

Walls should be made from uneven plaster or wide planks of rough timber, perhaps fixed horizontally. Go for white with woodwork in a vivid contrast like red or blue, or try an even bolder scheme such as pale pink walls with sea-green skirtings and architraves.

For authenticity, the floor should be a cold, hard surface such as marble, stone or ceramic tiles; cheaper materials like oiled concrete or painted cement tiles would also look right, as well as being just as easy to look after and equally hardwearing. Unless you have underfloor central heating, however, for which these materials are ideal, you may want something more comfortable to walk on, so settle for timber floorboards either painted white or given a scrubbed, weathered look. Tiles (glazed or unglazed) are an important design element though, so be generous with their use in the bathroom and kitchen, perhaps on the work-top and splashback instead of the floor.

Shutters in a simple fretwork or lattice pattern are common in sunny countries; to camouflage an ugly view, choose (or make) some with a very open design to let in light, and leave them permanently closed. At night, a plain roller blind in the same colour as the

RIGHT Tropical styling adapts itself perfectly to settings on the edge of the garden. In this restful dining corner of a verandah, crisp fabrics, painted wicker chairs, and a mass of greenery combine to good effect.

- To make decorative latticed shutters, mount suitable lengths of timber garden trellis (look for the expandable kind) on to two frames made to the required size, then add hinges and hang; for an even easier treatment, fix a single panel assembled in the same way over the whole window, hinging it at the top to give access. A similar panel would camouflage a radiator or sound system (rather than hiding it completely), while a larger version would make a subtle, unobtrusive room divider.

- Put together a striking collection of scatter cushions by covering a number of pads of the same size and shape (everyday bed pillows work well) in striped deck-chair canvas, using a wide variety of colours and patterns. Make each cushion different, and plan them so that when they're massed together, some stripes run vertically and some horizontally.

RIGHT To create a cool tropical look, choose a colour scheme of pure white and palest mint green, accessorized with natural materials like wood and wicker. In this summery bathroom, inexpensive garden trellis covers the window as well as the door, which is softened with gauzy curtains.

walls will afford the necessary privacy. Alternatively, hang light-weight, unlined curtains of unbleached cotton or linen, maybe with a border of peasant embroidery; a bright gaudy print featuring tropical fruit, flowers or birds would make pretty curtains too, or a tablecloth or bedspread, but don't use anything so garish too widely – in this case, once is probably enough.

Rooms should be sparsely furnished with large, sturdy, rustic pieces in dark or painted wood rather than delicate or grand ones with a naturally pale finish; look for homely second-hand items or new whitewood pieces that you can paint in white or a suitably florid colour. For multi-purpose storage, find large freestanding cupboards along the lines of a French armoire (old wardrobes might do the trick) or display things on thick, open shelves. Choose simple, low seating with generous proportions, like a huge, square sofa, a built-in banquette or an ordinary divan with a tailored cover and a bank of multicoloured cushions; upholstery fabrics should be crisp, natural ones that can be washed, such as sailcloth or canvas. For a really fresh look that's also inexpensive, go for tough deck-chair canvas in plain colours or cheerful stripes. Try to find occasional chairs made from wide slats of timber softened with plump seat and back pads, or provide extra seating in the form of a wooden garden bench, again with a comfortable squab cushion tied in place.

Give the effect of abundant greenery by massing lush ferns and big flowering plants in every room. If you have a heated greenhouse or conservatory (or a great deal of money) you can also fill your house with tropical flowers such as orchids, frangipani and bougainvillaea. Otherwise cheat by substituting good-quality silk blooms that look uncannily real, or settle for equally showy, but rather more domestic (and therefore cheaper), species that your budget can accommodate. Provide additional 'vegetation' in the form of pineapples, figs, limes, melons and bananas, heaped in a vivid green or yellow pottery bowl.

It's important not to overdo the accessories, but you could suggest an oceanside existence by displaying a collection of exquisite shells, bleached driftwood or intricately shaped coral, all of which can be bought from specialist shops if visiting a hot sandy beach is seldom on your holiday agenda. Adorn your walls with a colourful woven hanging instead of prints or paintings, or make your own by stretching a suitable fabric (a traditional kanga, perhaps) over a wooden frame. To add a witty finishing touch, install a brilliantly plumed bird – a parrot or even a budgerigar – that will conjure up exotic tropical fantasies.

FAR LEFT A collection of pottery glazed in colours reminiscent of the sea is set off against a neutral background of roughly plastered white walls, ceiling beams and tiled wash-basin surround in this pretty cloakroom.

BELOW Suggest the nearness of the ocean by painting or staining all your woodwork in a deep sea-blue. In this simple kitchen, meals are served on brightly painted native pottery, and a straw hat lies on the window sill, ready to offer protection against the noon-day sun.

Colonial

The colonial look is very much a mixture of the exotic and the familiar, an appealing cross between the cultures, crafts and decorating conventions of a far-away, usually tropical, country, and those imported by the European people who settled there.

CREATING THE LOOK

Colonial colours are pale and interesting rather than vivid and intense, and materials are left in their natural state whenever possible; choose plain cream walls with woodwork picked out in a muted grey-green or eau-de-Nil for just the right effect. Floors should be made from stripped timber, either left alone or lightly stained, then waxed, but if this is too costly or difficult to lay, cork tiles will do, since they have the appropriate texture and colour.

Louvred shutters in natural wood are one of the main elements of this style, perhaps because the way they filter the light somehow suggests the tropics even when the temperature outside is near freezing. Alternatively, look for wooden venetian blinds or those made from cane or pinoleum that roll up from the bottom. If you want a softer window treatment, hang filmy white curtains (use muslin or gauze) from a wooden pole; to give the impression of billowing in a warm breeze, they should be very generously gathered, so buy enough fabric to make them about three times the width of the window. Curtains like these also look charming when they droop slightly on to the floor; allow a little extra length if this fashion appeals to you.

Colonial furniture is never ponderous or fussy, so search out simple, light pieces in cane, wicker, bamboo and natural wood; darker timbers like mahogany can look right too because they grow in just the kind of hot, moist climate we associate with this style. Make sure there are plenty of small tables that you can cover with a lacy white cloth when you want to serve cooling glasses of punch and iced tea. Banish over-stuffed upholstery in favour of chairs and sofas with a wood or wicker frame and deep squashy cushions covered in crisp cream or white fabric – not silk, brocade or velvet. If you can find one, a traditional

RIGHT *Elegant eighteenth-century furnishings combine with terracotta floor tiles, cream washed walls, streaming sunlight and verdant foliage to produce a charming hybrid style.*

• Louvred shutters never date like passing fashions in curtains or blinds, and they look good with a wide range of furnishing styles; buy them new, or look for old ones at an architectural salvage yard. In addition to their use as a window covering, louvre panels make excellent cupboard or wardrobe doors, and can even be used as an internal door on a kitchen or utility room where noise is not a problem. Roll-up cane blinds are equally versatile; if you're always banging your head on open cupboard doors in your kitchen, use these instead to conceal clutter without taking up any space.

• For attractive dress curtains that involve few sewing skills, buy a length of filmy white material a little longer than twice the height of your window, plus its width, then hem just the ends, leaving the selvedges as they are. Twist the middle of the fabric loosely around a wooden curtain pole fixed above the window-frame, letting the material fall to the ground in soft folds at either side of the window. Fit a plain roller blind as well to block out the glaring midday sun and the neighbours' view when necessary.

planter's chair would add a really authentic touch to your room; made of wood with a high back, these have exceptionally long arms on which the plantation master could support his legs while his manservant tugged off his high boots.

In hot, humid places, every bed is raised high off the ground to discourage insects from crawling in with the occupant, as well as to allow air to circulate underneath. To give the effect of a mosquito net and to dress your bed prettily at the same time, suspend a length of muslin across the top from a hook fixed into the ceiling. Alternatively, make a canopy (from *canopeum*, Latin for mosquito net) by draping one end of the muslin over a curtain pole fixed high on the wall behind the head of the bed, extending the fabric along the bed lengthways, then draping the other end over the foot. Reinforce the cool, fresh look by choosing sheets and pillowcases in pure white cotton or natural linen.

Create a miniature jungle by investing in lots of potted palms and yuccas, grouping floor-

FAR LEFT The occupant of this ascetic bedroom can look out through large Georgian windows on to a lush tropical forest. As well as keeping insects at bay, the high bed with its pretty turned posts leaves the polished timber floor visually uncluttered, while its lacy white counterpane adds a softening touch.

LEFT A conservatory-like extension is the ideal place to create an exotic jungle-inspired scheme. This stone-floored kitchen with its brilliant white brick walls makes an ideal setting for the natural polished timber of a purpose-built, freestanding storage cupboard, and the leafy potted plants that surround it. Note the ingenious pull-out willow baskets that allow air to circulate freely around their contents.

standing specimens together and displaying smaller ones nearby in baskets and wooden tubs. To increase the effect, hang bamboo birdcages full of trailing plants from wall- or ceiling-fixed brackets directly above them. Because of the humidity, bathrooms make excellent mini-conservatories; search out a collection of cane plant stands that will also hold baskets of soap and toiletries.

A creamy cotton hammock with a delicate lacy edge shouldn't be hidden away until it can be used outdoors in summer – suspend it across a corner of your bedroom to put you in mind of sunny days all the year round. Similarly, a traditional oiled paper parasol would look enchanting simply opened out on the floor – or place it against the wall in front of a small table lamp so that it filters the light softly. DIY enthusiasts could cut down the handle to make a beautiful shade for a wall- or ceiling-mounted fitting. Supplement plain ceramic or brass table lights with glass-covered hurricane lamps that will give your rooms a romantic glow at any time and serve you well in case of a power cut. Finally, make every attempt to install that ultimate Somerset Maugham accessory, a large ceiling fan; modern electric ones are extremely useful as they do much more than provide a cool breeze. When the central heating goes on, they can also be adjusted to force the rising warm air back down into the room, thus reducing the demand on the heating system and saving money.

LEFT *These traditional mahogany and porcelain bathroom fittings have been given a colonial look by surrounding them with rich earth colours like rust, gold and sand, and adding appropriate accessories such as a marble plinth, verandah-like cane furniture, an oriental rug and, on the wall, an intrepid galleon negotiating uncharted waters.*

Oriental

*C*ool, spare and serene, an oriental room is character-ized by large areas of plain white with dramatic touches of marigold yellow, lacquer red and black. Straight lines and geometrical shapes dominate, and furnishings, objects and pictures are arranged asymmetrically. Instead of small rooms divided by brick walls, oriental houses often have a single open space; when necessary, activ-ity areas are defined with sliding screens, an idea – and a style – that people living in one room might like to copy.

CREATING THE LOOK

Start with smooth, non-shiny, white walls and a contrasting floor – perhaps black tiles or dark-stained wood, with several mats on top; to be really authentic, these should be of the genuine *tatami* variety, made from rice straw covered with fragrant rush, and measuring 90 × 180cm (3 × 6ft) and 5cm (2in) thick (large enough to accommodate one per-son lying down or two people standing). Traditionally, these were used as chairs, tables and beds as well as floor coverings, and at one time rooms were even de-scribed by the number that would fit in – six-mat rooms, eight-mat rooms etc. *Tatami* mats are not

easy to find in the West, however, and are very expensive, so use the cheap, much thinner ones bound with green tape that have approxi-mately the same dimensions and are fairly widely available (often at seaside resorts).

Made from delicate translucent paper stretched over a slim, grid-shaped wooden frame, Japanese *shoji* screens are sold at specialist shops, but anyone with basic car-pentry skills would find them easy to put together; get the paper from an artist's supplier. Alternatively, imitate the effect of another tradi-tional screen, the *sudare*, with a cane or wooden slatted blind that rolls up from the bottom; to act as room dividers, these would have to be unusually long, so you may have to order them specially. Make your screens movable so you can alter the look and the function of your space at will, or use them as permanent barriers, separating an eating from a cook-ing area, or enclosing a quiet study corner in a bedroom. Another subtle way to suggest different

RIGHT Give a featureless room a Japanese flavour by painting the walls white and defining activity areas with screens made from strips of black-painted timber. Add low furniture in similarly stark colours.

- Where privacy is necessary (in a bathroom, for instance), or when you want to conceal an unattractive view, replace ordinary window glass with the plain translucent or frosted variety. If it won't interfere with the window mechanism, make this look like a traditional screen by glueing thin strips of wood over the surface in a pattern of squares. To achieve a similar effect with less trouble, make a hinged window panel of timber strips laid in a grid pattern, or stretch fine white fabric over the frame.

RIGHT In this authentic Japanese house, sliding screens made from translucent paper take the place of curtains or blinds, and conventional Western furniture mixes comfortably with traditional, locally made designs. Although the main area is floored with black slate, the raised seating platform near the window is covered with rectangular tatami mats.

'rooms' is by changing the floor level slightly, building a low platform for the dining or seating area.

Curtains don't really suit this idiom, so replace them with shutters made in the same design as your screens – or just stand a screen in front of your window when you want it covered. For a more conventional treatment, fit unadorned roman blinds, which give the right linear, graphic effect.

Many oriental rooms stand almost empty much of the time, with equipment – and even furniture such as tables and floor cushions – being kept in concealed cupboards until needed. This approach requires plenty of storage capacity, though, so install deep fitted units right across one wall, with sliding doors that are plain white or, again, made to match your screens. Even if you don't want quite such a disciplined look, a storage unit of this size might be a better idea than several small freestanding or built-in items which could look bitty.

People tend to sit on or near the floor in an oriental house (which is why shoes are removed at the door), so choose a simple, low sofa or several large flat cushions. Tables should be equally low, and a large sturdy one that holds cups of coffee and magazines during the day can, with individual floor cushions placed around it, serve as a dining table in the evening. Give all hard surfaces a high, lacquer-like shine; several coats of gloss and a great deal of careful rubbing down in between them should do the trick.

This clean, practical, no-fuss style is ideal for kitchens, and a range of units in plain black would set the scene perfectly, especially if you add touches of red detailing and display appropriate accessories like a rush steamer, a wok and a Chinese tea set. Give the bathroom a similarly sleek, uncluttered look by installing wall-mounted fittings to keep the floor clear, and fixing a low shelf of well-sealed wooden duck-boarding all around, or just across one wall, to provide seating and useful storage capacity as well. Instead of an ordinary shallow, rectangular bath, go for a deep, square one like the oriental tubs intended for relaxation rather than cleanliness, and replace ordinary towel rails with black-painted dowelling, fixed in straight rows or in a classic grid pattern.

One Japanese furnishing item that has become widely popular is

BELOW Transform a boring kitchen into an exotic oriental one by devising a stylish black-and-white treatment for most of th design elements, then painting the walls in dramatic lacquer red. Here, two cleverly designed (but very simple) curtain panels have been made from translucent white fabric, then given a dark border to resemble shoji screens.

the futon, a thick mattress made from layers of cotton wadding. Rolled up and hidden away during the day, this is laid on the floor at bed time. The number of layers it contains determines the degree of comfort it offers; clearly, thinner ones are easier to store and handle, while thicker ones are softer to sleep on. Whatever weight you choose, be sure to air it regularly –

you lose up to half a litre (a pint) of moisture in perspiration every night, so there's a very real danger of mildew. Traditionally, futons are used only as mattresses, but in the West we have developed a dual-purpose version with a hinged base that converts into a sofa during the day; use this design in a bedsitter, or to accommodate occasional guests.

ABOVE Two high slatted screens painted with lacquer-like black gloss set off the toilet and bidet in this spacious bathroom, and provide hanging capacity for bath towels at the same time. Underneath the projecting basin, a neat semi-circular rail copes with hand towels.

To reinforce the tranquil atmosphere, limit yourself to a small but very carefully chosen collection of accessories. Lighting, for example, should come from subtle, fairly low-placed sources such as simple table lamps with coolie shades or plain opal glass wall fittings – try putting a *shoji* screen in front of one of these for a soft, flattering glow. An oriental room is the ideal place for the ubiquitous round paper shade with a wire or bamboo frame, perhaps hung low over a table; this must be white, though, never coloured, to give the right effect and to ensure that the illumination looks natural. Find a beautiful lacquer tray, a delicate fan or a vividly coloured kite to hang on the wall, or display a single, exquisite kimono by suspending it from a length of dowelling slotted through the arms. Search out one or two pieces of pottery that are genuinely oriental or at least oriental in feeling, and display them against a contrasting background for maximum impact. For green interest, a bonsai plant (or miniature tree) would look perfect, or take inspiration from *ikebana*, the Japanese art of flower arranging in which the components are grouped (alone or with twigs or polished stones) in the shape of a triangle. To add a sculptural element and increase heating efficiency at the same time, replace conventional radiators with wall-mounted vertical ones in striking designs, or use freestanding models that can be positioned in the middle of the floor to act as room dividers.

● An ordinary mattress without a divan base makes an ideal low oriental bed, but it should never be placed directly on the ground because it will quickly become damp from lack of ventilation. Instead, make an inexpensive base consisting of a row of timber battens fixed across a rudimentary frame, then paint this to match the floor covering.

LEFT If your futon is to be left in place permanently, construct a ventilated timber base for it, which you can then camouflage with a coat of dark-coloured paint; here, the bright yellow bedding appears to float freely in space. As an appropriately unfussy window covering, choose white Venetian blinds, which are readily available and comparatively inexpensive.

Indian

When we think of Indian homes, we tend to picture either mud huts with earth floors or princely palaces decked out in gold, marble and mosaic. In fact, there is no single, widespread style of decoration we can adapt directly, but it is possible to suggest the atmosphere of the subcontinent by employing the rich and varied collection of handicrafts and textiles that are made for the export market.

CREATING THE LOOK

You'll need a fairly plain background for Indian artefacts, which are often extravagantly patterned or brilliantly hued (a fact that inspired Diana Vreeland, one-time editor of American *Vogue*, to remark that 'pink is the navy blue of India'), so choose solid colours for your walls and floors.

Begin by investigating the enormous and varied range of Indian textiles, from unbleached cotton, silk and wool to bright patchwork and appliqué from Gujarat, embroidered crewelwork from Kashmir and intricate mirrorwork from Rajasthan, which consists of tiny pieces of mirror glass set into needlework motifs. Choose curtains in homespun Gandhi cloth, raw silk or thick, slubby cotton, which comes in an enormous variety of colours, and can be used for loose covers as well. For a subtle, sophisticated effect, go for upholstery in heavy natural cotton, or a hard-wearing cotton/silk mix, and add beautifully decorated cushions or those made from hand-printed fabrics in traditional patterns. For a wide range of suitable designs, search out a shop that sells lengths of sari material, which might also make delicate, filmy curtains for a small window.

India has a large rug-making industry, producing flat woven cotton dhurries, woollen druggets and kelims that are sold all over the world. In ordinary homes, these are used not only as floor coverings, but also as tablecloths and wall hangings – and even as a form of padding over the *charpoi*, a primitive bed made from string stretched over a wooden frame. Using this for inspiration, make an exotic cover for a low divan by laying a fairly lightweight dhurrie on top.

RIGHT Originally made by nomadic tribes, kelims were woven from finest-quality wool to make them durable enough for constant use and frequent folding. Display perfect specimens on the floor or the wall, and rescue sound portions of damaged ones to make cushion – or even chair – covers.

● Indian dhurries come in a huge assortment of designs, weights and prices, the heaviest ones with the most complex patterns being much more expensive than the light, simple striped examples at the other end of the market. These represent such good value that you could even buy one or two specially to cut up for cushion covers – or use a colourful dhurrie instead of fabric to upholster a padded stool or pouffe, or even a small chair if there is enough material and you have the necessary skills and equipment. For an unusual window treatment, replace ordinary curtains with a pair of matching dhurries. To do this, stitch a length of heading tape along one end of each rug, then hang them from rings on a stout pole, making sure the brackets are fixed securely enough to take the strain.

RIGHT Among the most popular Indian handicrafts are painted tinware, hand-turned and decorated wooden boxes, embroidered textiles, and patterned brass articles.

FAR RIGHT A tiny hall corner has been given drama and interest with the addition of this exquisite table and chair inlaid with mother-of-pearl chips, an exotic wallhanging.

Furniture should be made from elaborately carved rosewood, or a similarly dark timber; some of the finest pieces are inlaid with mother-of-pearl. Brass-topped tables on a collapsible round wooden base often find their way into junk shops; use one as it is, or remove the top to make a huge tray, perhaps to display a lamp or a collection of brass bowls or candlesticks. As well as plain brass, try to find one or two pieces enamelled in brilliant turquoise or red. Other craft items worth looking for are papier-mâché boxes from Kashmir and traditional paintings and miniatures, either good-quality copies of old ones or new originals. To create the atmosphere of India instantly, light some fragrant joss sticks.

PERIOD STYLE

---

*T*hroughout every period in history, people have used earlier ages as a rich source of decorating ideas and influences. Borrow freely from the style that holds the strongest appeal for you, but don't become too obsessed with creating rooms that are authentic in every detail: we often have very blurred visual perceptions of the past, and a historically perfect scheme might look nothing like we imagine it. What's more important is that our homes are for living in, not just looking at, so convenience and comfort should never be sacrificed to dry scholarship.

Early English

Before the eighteenth century, people's attitudes towards furnishings were very different from ours; comfort was not high on the list of priorities, status and fine craftsmanship being considered far more important. Compared to our own, their rooms were somewhat spartan, but they had a tranquil simplicity from which we can learn much.

SETTING THE SCENE

The first function of almost all household furnishings was to keep out the cold; to this end, walls were either panelled or hung with tapestries, both of which would also make an excellent disguise for damaged or uneven plaster in modern homes, as well as providing efficient sound insulation. We tend to think of old panelling as being made from very dark oak, but this effect is usually the result of ageing; although never pale, its original colour would have been rather lighter in tone. Try to find a supplier of reproduction panelling (which is fairly expensive), or make your own using sheets of MDF (medium density fibreboard) and strips of architectural moulding. Paint it with a flat dark colour, or employ the specialist paint technique of graining to make it look like wood.

In the absence of priceless tapestries, cover large expanses of wall with panels of suitable fabric (crewelwork or flamestitch, perhaps, or a design that has been woven to look like tapestry), hung by a pole or stretched over a frame. Alternatively, put up a collection of rugs in suitably rich, muted colours: oriental designs with a low pile, for example, or flat-weave Indian rugs, which are widely available and not too expensive. In most homes, any kind of rug would have been much too costly to lay on the floor; a beautiful specimen was more likely to be draped over a table, then covered with a lace-trimmed linen cloth at meal times. This style is still popular in Holland and Belgium, where even restaurant tables are covered with carpets and suitable ones are for sale in street markets and shops; if the Low Countries are not on your itinerary, however, use any appropriately sized rug that is dark in colour and light in weight.

RIGHT Named after the Kent house for which it was first made, a Knole sofa with its deep cushions and adjustable ends represents the most advanced design thinking of this age. Tables would be covered with richly hued rugs, on which backgammon and bagatelle could be played.

- Traditional rush mats are still made, but they're neither easy to find nor cheap, so substitute those woven from sea grass, coconut fibre (coir) or sisal, which are imported from the Far East. If necessary, these can be stitched together to make a large mat, but remember that this material collects dirt and dust underneath, so make sure you can lift it easily for cleaning. To prevent your mats from drying out in a centrally heated room, moisten them with water from time to time using a plant sprayer.

RIGHT A really authentic floor should be made of dark-stained timber, with mats on top that are woven from thick rushes plaited into strips, then stitched together. At this time, only the head of the household or an important guest would warrant an arm chair; lowlier souls would be allotted a side chair or even a backless stool.

If you want to achieve an authentic look you'll have to forgo fitted carpets – floors should be made from wood that has been given a medium or dark stain, then waxed. Originally, this was covered with rush matting, then sprinkled with handfuls of sweet-smelling herbs.

Very grand homes might have had damask or figured velvet curtains, but in ordinary rooms window coverings were not there for ornament, or even insulation (as windows were very small), but just to keep out the sun. Plain shutters were common, as were simple unlined curtains made from natural wool or linen and cut to fit the window exactly rather than fall to the floor. These were hung by iron rings (sewn directly to the fabric) from an iron pole curved at the ends to hold the material in position. For a realistic touch, hang a single curtain, wide enough to pull right across the glass – divided curtains did not become

ABOVE Panelling would have been left in its natural, medium-oak colour, or painted a rich, sombre shade like deep green. For illumination, rooms as grand as this one would have depended on a huge, blazing fire supplemented by a collection of beeswax candles and, often, a simple, central chandelier.

• It would clearly be impractical to depend on candles for everyday lighting, but consider adding drama to special occasions (a supper or birthday party maybe, or Christmas dinner) by switching off the electric lights altogether and using only a chandelier that takes real candles, or wall sconces supplemented by individual candles on the table.

popular until the end of the seventeenth century. If any of your windows are awkwardly shaped or located very near a corner, this treatment could be ideal.

To look right, lighting should be soft and unobtrusive; search out several heavy candlesticks or sconces made from pewter or wood, and add thick candles – originally, these would have been made from beeswax, but plain white altar candles will work just as well. For more workaday illumination, choose the plainest wall and table lights you can find.

APPLYING THE STYLE
Most furniture was made from solid oak, turned and elaborately carved in patterns like the characteristic barley-sugar twist. Common items were huge refectory tables, and boxes, chests and coffers, which were used not only for storage, but also as display surfaces and, with the addition of a cushion, as extra seating. Many rooms had a sturdy corner cupboard, either freestanding or built into the panelling, which sometimes extended the entire height of the room. There would also be a large open cupboard or buffet for displaying drinking vessels and plates made from carved wood or pewter – earthenware was not produced cheaply enough for common use, or in any great quantity, until the eighteenth century.

When it comes to seating, few of us would find authentic pieces comfortable enough; not only was comfort considered unimportant, but the clothing of the time was

RIGHT The large, stone-floored kitchen at Cotehele in Cornwall, an imposing house built between 1485 and 1627 that has recently been restored and opened to the public by the National Trust. Note the large collection of pewter dishes that were used for both serving and eating before the widespread availability of earthenware.

thick enough on its own to provide a good layer of padding. A wooden settle that kept out draughts with its high back and winged ends was very typical; even with a squab cushion, such a piece would be too unyielding to serve as the main seating in any room, but it might be useful in a hall or large kitchen. Early settles would have been positioned against a wall, but set across the middle of the floor, they could be very useful for separating the living room or kitchen from the dining area or providing a corner for quiet study.

One seating design that would work extremely well in modern rooms is the Knole sofa, whose equally high back and sides had a layer of padding over the frame, and an iron ratchet that made it possible for the sides to drop down. Reproduction Knole sofas are widely available, but these days the ratchet has usually been replaced by thick tassels anchored around large turned knobs at each corner. When upholstering furniture, remember that early fabrics were woven in narrow widths of about 60cm (2ft), so it was necessary to seam several of these together to extend across the back of a sofa; the seams were then disguised with ribbon or braid. Other appropriate designs are large, high wing chairs, Windsor chairs, carved day-beds with caned seats and backs, and small stools; 'backstools' were hard chairs without arms, much like our dining chairs, that had slung leather seats anchored to the frame with brass studs, or cushions on top of rigid wooden seats.

Each bedroom would have contained a chest, a small chair or stool, and a cupboard with shelves inside for clothes (but no mirror, since these were too rare and expensive for the average home), but the most dominant feature of the room by far was the massive, high bed with a four-poster frame from which tapestries or curtains were hung to keep out the cold. If you have a big enough budget – and a high enough room – you can install a reproduction four-poster, ready-made or in self-assembly form, which is slightly less costly. Alternatively, settle for a half-tester bed, which has fabric hanging at its head only. For a much more subtle touch, replace a standard headboard with a length of tapestry-like fabric gathered gently and hung by rings from a thick brass or dark wooden pole fixed into the wall above the bed.

Whatever style you choose for your bed, borrow a space-saving idea from early English bedrooms and buy or make a small trundle bed that rolls away underneath it when not in use. This can be pressed into service when overnight guests arrive, either by accommodating one of them directly, or by providing sleeping space for a child, whose room is then freed for the visitor.

To add a charming touch and encourage a peaceful night's sleep, tie a bunch of fragrant herbs or a clove-studded orange pomander to your bedpost with a length of plain ribbon.

- If you have neither the money nor the space for an authentic four-poster bed, cheat by suspending gathered fabric on rings from ceiling-fixed curtain poles or lengths of thick dowelling, either all around the bed, or only at its head for a half-tester effect. Slot your poles directly into sturdy brackets, or suspend them from thick chains, but make sure that all fixing is done into joists or beams that can support the weight of the fabric.

FAR LEFT In this sumptuous bedchamber, the floor has been close covered with rush matting, which acts as insulation and provides a backdrop for precious oriental rugs. The rich tapestries that adorn the walls and the elaborate silken curtains on the four-poster bed were also designed originally to keep out the cold; in poorer homes, the same tactics were employed using less costly materials.

Georgian and Regency

During the eighteenth and early nineteenth centuries, many furnishing styles went in and out of vogue, from swirly, over-the-top rococo to exuberant chinoiserie and exotic Egyptian. The look that had the most lasting influence, though, and the one associated most strongly with this period, is formal, elegant neo-classicism, which was brought back to England by fashionable aristocrats who had visited Italy on their statutory Grand Tour, and been profoundly affected by its art and architecture. Many people consider this the era to have inspired the finest design and craftsmanship, with its emphasis on symmetry, perfect proportions, delicate, restrained shapes, and cool, soft colours like pea green and stone, or light, bright ones such as acid yellow and sky blue. Appearance was still much more important than comfort or convenience, however, so keep this in mind when you decide how faithfully to reproduce this look.

SETTING THE SCENE

Georgian walls were rarely perfectly plain; plaster or panelling should be painted, marbled or colour-washed – or choose wallpaper in a quiet stripe (in reception rooms), or a delicate floral pattern (in bedrooms). Give doors and woodwork a subtle eggshell finish; shiny gloss bears no resemblance to any eighteenth-century finish. 'Gothick', one of the variations of Georgian style, was characterized by ecclesiastical touches like pointed arches, plaster niches and intricate, wedding-cake detailing at cornice level.

Surprisingly, fitted carpet is perfectly suitable for Georgian rooms, since this kind of flooring – achieved by stitching together narrow strips of carpeting – was widely used. The other possibility is natural floorboards with a large area rug, probably oriental, in the middle; in houses of the time, all the furniture would have been arranged stiffly around the edges of a room, leaving the rug (or

RIGHT This cool Georgian corner features an imposing stone bust framed by softly draped curtains in the scheme's dominant grey-green colour. Note the 'mosaic' table whose classical motifs are actually painted on.

- Stark white radiators will add a jarring note to your carefully created period interior, so give them the same paint treatment as your walls – a solid colour, or a special finish such as marbling or graining. Although ordinary white emulsion will yellow as a result of high temperatures, colours are comparatively unaffected, so just rub down the radiator with fine sandpaper to provide a key, then apply your finish.

- For a *trompe-l'oeil* Gothick cornice, search out a stencil border in a suitable design of small arches or delicate tracery, then fill it in using opaque white paint to create the effect of solid plaster.

RIGHT Electricity has been banished from this exquisite Regency room altogether; at night, an original Murano glass chandelier provides illumination. The subtle, but very effective, decorating elements include an unassuming trellis-patterned wallpaper, a collection of Adam Buck transfer china and a lovingly hand-grained finish on the window panelling and shutters.

the central section of the carpet) uncovered.

Window dressings should be light and flimsy, since they were there to soften the lines of the window as well as to filter the sunlight. Fix ordinary drawn curtains, or corded festoon blinds with a pretty pelmet or valance, in delicate silky fabrics or thin cottons; a very popular choice was *toile de Jouy*, a French chintz printed with sweeping pastoral scenes in a single colour on a white ground, and you should be able to find this fairly easily in any shop that stocks a comprehensive range of furnishing materials.

This was the golden age of Chippendale, Sheraton and Hepplewhite, a flowering of skill and craftsmanship occasioned largely by the lifting of import duties on beautifully grained West Indian hardwoods such as satinwood and light-coloured mahogany. Shapes were refined and graceful, and surfaces were adorned with exquisite marquetry, intricate carving and delicate gilding. Legs on early Georgian furniture were curved in the cabriole shape associated with the Queen Anne period immediately previous, but later, in sympathy with the classical feeling, legs were plain and tapering and often took the form of slender fluted columns.

When it comes to lighting, look for table fittings with bases in this typically classic shape, and add several candles in similarly designed holders, plus special shades supported on brass carriers that lower them as the candle burns

down. If you can manage the expense, a reproduction (or an original) candelabrum would look wonderful on a dining table or sideboard. Wall sconces would also add an authentic touch, as would a *girandole*, a candle holder that is attached to a wall-hung mirror so the sparkling effect is multiplied.

The technology for making mirrors of a reasonable size, in large numbers, and at an affordable price, was developed for the first time in the eighteenth century, and they were a very popular accessory, valued especially for their ability to make rooms look larger and enhance any available light, thus helping to relieve the general gloom that prevailed in houses before the invention of electricity. A particularly ingenious style was the circular convex wall mirror that worked on the same principle as a wide-angle lens to increase the apparent size of a room in its reflection.

As well as formal portraits and landscapes, botanical prints were frequently hung on the wall, as were cut-out or drawn silhouettes of either a full figure or a head and shoulders only. It was at this time that cut flowers were first brought indoors, and grouped in huge, grand, symmetrical shapes, often slightly broken by trailing greenery such as ivy. An arrangement of this kind would be made up of mixed blooms from the herbaceous border like roses, phlox, delphiniums, mock orange blossom and stock, and displayed in a vase shaped like a classical urn.

LEFT Bold Regency-stripe wallpaper dominates this striking, yet eminently practical pied-à-terre. *To avoid a cluttered look, and to remain faithful to the convention of the period, the furniture has been lined up against the walls, leaving the central floor area clear. To the right, a sleeping alcove is set off with curtains and matching swagged pelmet in a related, but quieter, stripe, with plain white under-drapes; at the window, the fabrics are reversed so that the festoon blind is striped and the curtains are white. The velvet-pile carpet is a soft terracotta colour throughout, and the walls around the bed have been painted with the same warm shade.*

RIGHT *Very different from the restraint of neo-classicism, the florid rococo style was also popular during the eighteenth century. Combining elements of both idioms, this room has a warm, lively feeling that comes largely from the glittering gilt on the elaborate console table, the intricate candlesticks and sconces, and the highly decorated girandole mirror.*

FAR RIGHT *Before the invention of chemical dyes, chintzes were coloured with subtly hued vegetables pigments; reminiscent of early designs, this modern one transforms a small, boxy bedroom into a floral fantasy. The material itself has been made up into a festoon blind, dress curtains and matching coverlet, while its exuberant blooms provided inspiration for the hand-painted decorations on the bed, the chair and the wall.*

APPLYING THE STYLE

Although entertaining and family life would have been centred around the living room, little emphasis was placed on relaxation; even with chairs, the frame was the most important part, so as much of it was exposed as possible, light padding being added only where absolutely necessary.

Sofas, where they existed, offered little more concession to comfort, since they often took the form of a row of chairs fastened together, or an unyielding couch called a day-bed, with flat, rigid end panels softened slightly by round bolsters. Other common seating items were the *chaise-longue*, which had one high side and a gently curved back, and the window seat, which at this period was freestanding, like a stool with low ends or a small backless sofa; this item came into common use when window glass was manufactured in large panes for the first time. To look right, chairs and sofas should be covered in a fine, light material such as silk, or its modern – and much more practical – equivalent, Dupion. To protect seating from dirt and dust, rudimentary loose covers made from checked or striped cotton might have been tied on, but these would be removed when the room was to be used for a formal occasion.

One furnishing item that has no place in a Georgian drawing room is the coffee table – a strictly twentieth-century invention. Substitute a small, high, round one on which you can play whist, or serve tea in the elegant creamware china that was so popular at the end of the eighteenth century, with its graceful shapes, translucent glaze and pretty pierced edges.

In the bedroom, clothes would not have been hung up, but folded in a large press; small items were kept in a high, narrow chest of drawers called a tallboy. Pride of

- If you are lucky enough to acquire an antique clothes press, don't chop out the drawers with the intention of converting it into a wardrobe; leave it in its original condition, and supplement it with unobtrusive fitted units for hanging garments, painted to match the walls, and perhaps trimmed with subtle, Georgian-inspired detailing such as moulding or beading applied in rectangular panels.

place, however, was still given to the bed, which would sometimes be framed by an alcove or recess to emphasize its importance. There might be a valance and a canopy, but curtains were likely to be hung at the head only, in the half-tester style; to give your bed an authentic look, drape it with chintz in a dainty bird or flower pattern like the early ones that were imported from India.

BIEDERMEIER

One of the most charming furnishing trends of the eighteenth century, and one that has had an enormous influence on modern taste, was the Biedermeier style developed in Germany and Austria. Although it, too, was influenced by classical shapes and proportions, Biedermeier swept away much of the fussy detailing so popular elsewhere, and placed the emphasis firmly on comfort, informality and practicality. Rooms were simpler on the whole, with wooden floors and solid-colour walls against which a few good pictures could be displayed. Fabrics, too, were plain rather than patterned, and furniture was crafted from light fruit-wood or ash in graceful but uncluttered designs. The importance of comfortable seating was acknowledged, and a typical sitting room would contain a large, generously upholstered sofa, with a group of chairs and small tables in front of it. Windows were dressed with lightly gathered curtains, sometimes hung asymmetrically, without pelmets or heavy trimming.

RIGHT Decorated by a confirmed neo-Georgian, this elegant, formal bedroom has several archetypal elements of the style, notably the Pompeii-red and pea-green colour scheme and the columnar forms of the table legs, the lamp bases, the mirror surround and the detailing on the chest of drawers – even the radiator has a faux-column paint finish. The three sash windows are hung with simple curtains whose headings are concealed by contrasting white pelmets made from soft, gauzy fabric draped symmetrically and anchored with matching rosettes. On the bed is a plain throwover cover in an understated woven stripe.

Victorian

The Victorian period was a long one – over 60 years – and fashions in interior design, as in everything else, underwent several changes during that time. The style we tend to think of as Victorian, however, was the one in vogue towards the end of the nineteenth century – an opulent, cosy look that reflected the increased emphasis on home and family.

At its best, the rich decoration of Victorian rooms made them welcoming and comfortable, but at their most extreme, they could also be gloomy, suffocating and totally impractical, so it's important to adapt this style in a way that suits your home and your way of life.

SETTING THE SCENE
While we are forever trying to make our rooms look higher and larger, the Victorians made a conscious effort to create a warm, intimate atmosphere by breaking up large expanses of wall in order to lower the ceiling visually. The most radical approach was to divide the wall horizontally into several sections: the skirting board, which was sometimes as deep as 40cm (16in); the dado section, painted with shiny gloss over a relief-patterned wallpaper; the dado rail; the main wall area, co-vered with a patterned paper; the picture rail; the frieze (plain, decorated with relief patterns, or papered with a contrasting design); and finally, the cornice moulding, which could be very complex or even pierced. This elaborate treatment would overpower most modern rooms, though, so tone it down by fixing a modestly sized skirting, perhaps with a strip of decorative moulding on top, then papering the wall up to picture-rail height, and painting the frieze area above it to match the ceiling.

Although fitted carpets were still popular in the early part of the period, they fell out of favour in the wake of a mid-Victorian obsession with cleanliness; as a result of this, late-nineteenth-century rooms had polished floor-boards covered with rugs and carpets that could be taken up and beaten. Tiling was also popular in areas of heavy wear such as halls, where tiny multicoloured encaustic tiles would be laid in intricate patterns; although these are still made today, they are prohibitively expensive, so use bigger clay,

RIGHT *Deep, glowing colours and gracefully curving shapes give a strong Victorian feeling to the historically disparate furnishing elements in this inviting corner.*

- When choosing paint for a dado area, remember that textured surfaces often make colours look quite different to the way they appear on flat ones. Similarly, artificial light can alter colour dramatically, so be sure to test a small amount of your chosen hue *in situ* before you make up your mind.

- It is possible to restore a cornice whose details have become blurred from countless layers of paint and distemper, but it's a time-consuming and tedious job, so you'll have to see it as a labour of love. Use a steam sprayer to dampen the old surfaces, and let the moisture soak in thoroughly, then use a nail or toothbrush to work the excess material free. If it still won't come out, pick very gently at it with a bradawl.

ceramic or vinyl ones arranged in a simpler design.

The abolition of the window tax in 1851 meant that houses built after this time had much larger windows than ever before. Unfortunately, the fashion for heavy, voluminous curtains of velvet, brocade or plush, with elaborate trimmings such as pelmets and swags, meant that much of the available light was shut out. To achieve a similar look without plunging your home into darkness, fix your curtains on a suitable brass or wooden pole (not a plastic track) that is long enough for them to be pulled clear of the glass, and provide plain or tasselled tie-backs. Underneath the main curtains, to afford privacy and keep out soot, would be a sort of petticoat of gathered white cotton lace, or sometimes a plain white holland blind adorned with a strip of lace along the bottom. If you live in an old house that has large built-in shutters, consider abandoning formal curtains altogether, and hang only lace panels to soften the windows and prevent people from looking in during the day. To keep out draughts, fix a narrow curtain made from plush or chenille inside the front door.

Victorian rooms were arranged in an informal way, with furniture brought away from the walls and arranged in groups around a fireplace or large table. Individual items were much bigger, darker and heavier than they had been during the Georgian period, with the most popular woods being dark mahogany and rosewood;

- If you want to add a cornice or a ceiling rose to a featureless room, you can still buy them in traditional fibrous plaster, or choose reproductions made from polyurethane or polystyrene, which are light, strong and fairly convincing once they've been given a coat of paint. In addition, these modern copies are much easier for an amateur to install. If only part of your cornice is missing, a specialist firm will be able to replace it by taking a mould from an existing section.

LEFT Late nineteenth-century houses tend to be rich in architectural detailing; this modest entrance hall is adorned with carved balusters and newel posts and an elaborate ceiling, plus simple architraves, skirtings and dado rails.

shapes and surfaces were rounded with curvy detailing, and many items had graceful carbriole legs, an echo of the Queen Anne period, which was enjoying renewed popularity. If money is tight, set the tone with just one or two nice pieces; large ones are easier to find and may even be cheaper than more delicate ones, which are highly sought after because they suit small, modern rooms. It's also true that antiques like this compare favourably in price even now with good reproduction or modern designs.

APPLYING THE STYLE

A typical Victorian drawing room was largely organized around an elaborate fireplace, whose importance was emphasized by its complex decoration; many had a pelmet or fringe on top and curtains that drew across it when the fire wasn't lit. There would have been an embroidered screen in front, and a carved overmantel mirror with integral shelves and candle brackets. Staffordshire figures, called flat-back figures, which had relief decoration and painting only on the front, were made specially for displaying on the mantel.

It was at this period that the upholsterer's art reached its apotheosis, thanks to the invention of the coil spring in 1828. Chairs and sofas (like the characteristic chesterfield design) were covered in leather, velvet or linen, and deeply buttoned, their frames completely obscured under bulbous curves. Similar upholstery techniques were used to produce

RIGHT The cluttered look at its most appealing, with some degree of decoration on every available surface. Subtle, trellis-patterned wallpaper for example, provides a flattering background for the extensive collection of miniatures in this archetypal Victorian parlour, and the dark-stained floorboards are almost hidden by opulently layered oriental rugs and carpets. Massed displays of china figures, antique fans, painted boxes, and clocks jostle for room on the tables and the mantlepiece, while the floor area seems to be planted with a forest of cabriole legs. The cut-out figures guarding the marble fireplace are called companion pieces, and these were a fairly common decorating accessory. Note the simply gathered curtains, hung from an elegant, but unobtrusive, brass rail.

another very Victorian furnishing item, the ottoman – a heavily padded box adorned with braid, tassels or embroidery, that can be used not only for storage, but also as a footstool and an extra seat. A set (matching or not) of Victorian balloon-back dining chairs would be a practical purchase for any modern home, since their sprung seats make them equally suitable for use as occasional chairs. Whichever style you prefer, you'll want your seating to be comfortable and hardwearing as well as right for the period, so in this case choose good reproduction pieces rather than genuinely old ones that are often beyond repair.

For an authentic look, there should be a profusion of decorative objects like papier-mâché boxes and trays (black, painted with floral motifs to look like lac-

quer), china figures and framed photographs, plus a suitable cabinet to accommodate them: that quintessentially Victorian curiosity, the multi-shelved whatnot would be ideal. Drape every available surface – tables, dressers, chests and pianos – with scarves or shawls to give the effect of pattern layered upon pattern, and display a mass of close-grouped pictures; they can actually prove easier to find and less costly than a single large one, which has to be of excellent quality to stand on its own. Lighting should not be a problem since electricity was introduced during the 1880s and accurate reproduction fittings are fairly widely available; brass ones with glass shades will always look right. If you like to have flowers around, remember that a real Victorian arrangement containing brilliantly

RIGHT Generous bunches of real foliage – edible and otherwise – echo the relief pattern on the leafy green plates and serving dishes arranged on this large, sturdy dresser. Underneath are several rows of useful small drawers (you can find similar ones in second-hand shop-display fittings) that will accommodate cutlery, napkins, kitchen utensils, stationery and odds and ends like string, rubber bands, drawing pins and candles.

hued hot-house blooms such as gladioli, lilies and carnations might look garish, especially when set out, in the fashion of the day, in a silver, cut-glass or china vase, or displayed in an elaborate centre-piece with lighted candles.

No one in their right mind would want to re-create an im-practical, labour-intensive Victo-rian kitchen, but you can add a little period charm to a modern one without sacrificing any of its efficiency. Country-house living was at its peak of popularity at this time, and a country-house kitchen (see pp 22–24) would not have looked very different from one in a large town house. To achieve the right atmosphere, install a huge cast-iron range and banish purpose-made units; as a com-

promise, supplement a large dres-ser and table with low-level cupboards, perhaps extending along an entire wall, to hold less attractive equipment, then fix open shelves or glass-fronted cup-boards above. If you want more concealed storage, back the glass with gathered fabric in a printed cotton that can easily be taken down and washed.

Victorian bedrooms, although highly decorated by our standards, were still plainer than the main reception rooms. In terms of furn-iture, there would have been a marble-topped washstand on which was set out a ewer and basin, plus matching soap dish, beaker etc; this was sometimes hidden by a large screen that also provided a corner for dressing.

ABOVE Dominating many Victorian bedrooms was a high, wide bed like this plainish brass one draped with a beautiful, hand-crocheted coverlet. At its foot, a comfortably padded chaise provides the perfect place to curl up with a Gothic novel. A pretty-but-practical touch is the lace pelmet hung behind the marble-topped wash-stand to protect the wallpaper from accidental splashes.

For the first time, clothes were hung (rather than folded) in a capacious wardrobe, probably made from mahogany; today, many people prefer fitted storage units to these bulky freestanding ones, so they are reasonably easy to find in antique and second-hand shops, and relatively cheap. Look for one that has integral drawers and shelves as well as hanging space, or choose a separate chest of drawers. Once again, the bed should be large and high and made from iron and brass, or carved wood; don't go overboard with drapery, however, since the Victorian passion for hygiene dictated that it had to be easily removable for laundering. At this time, beds would have been hung with British-manufactured chintz, which was brighter than the earlier version from India due to advances in dye-making technology.

Creating a nineteenth-century nursery is surprisingly cost-effective, since in houses of the period most items of furniture – tables, sofas and so forth – would simply have been moved there when they outlived their usefulness in other rooms. Wallpaper and fabrics specially for children were the exception rather than the rule, but there was always a place for traditional toys, some of which were designed originally as teaching aids: a rocking horse to instruct young gentlemen in equestrian skills for example, or a doll's house full of scaled-down furnishings and equipment to school young ladies in the organization of domestic life.

LEFT In wealthy homes, the master bedroom might also act as a private sitting room, away from the noise and bustle of a large household. Here, at the end of the enormous four-poster bed, a collection of comfortable chairs and sofas has been arranged near the fireplace. Close by is a small round table for playing patience or dealing with correspondence, while to the right a freestanding cheval glass (an enlarged version of the pivoting dressing-table mirror) gives a full-length view for last-minute grooming checks. The room's main decorative element is the large-scale flowery chintz used for the sofa, the stool, the occasional chair, the cushions and the pouffe, as well as the bed's elaborate curtains, pelmet and valance.

- Ceramic tiles must be laid on a stable, level surface, so if your floor is uneven, you may need to put down a subfloor of hardboard or chipboard. If your bathroom is very large, and on an upper level, make sure the floor is strong enough to take what is bound to be considerable extra weight.

RIGHT *Converted from an existing bedroom, this spacious bathroom has been completely clad in ceramic tiles – plain ones on the floor and the walls, plus a picture-rail-height border of small mosaics arranged in a Greek key design. Marble was a popular material in Victorian bathrooms; here it forms a surround for the rectangular inset basin, and a platform for the traditional roll-top bath.*

FAR RIGHT *This formal, spare bathroom was inspired by the early, rather than the late Victorian period, and still retains some characteristics of the Georgian era, like the cool colour scheme, the neo-classical detailing on the basin pedestal, the filmy draped curtain, and the typical egg-and-dart border design at cornice level. Borrowed from the end of the century however, are the mahogany panelling around the bath, the elaborate brass shower fittings, and the small, dark and curvy table and chairs.*

Plumbed-in bathrooms first appeared after drainage and sewage systems were introduced in the 1870s; converted from extra bedrooms, these would have had white tiled floors or walls similarly clad, or panelled with marble. This kind of scheme is an excellent choice in a modern bathroom, since ceramic surfaces are just as practical now as they were then, and probably less expensive to achieve in real terms. Carry the look through by installing large fittings (plain white or decorated with delicate patterns) in suitable period shapes; a roll-top bath, for example, or an ordinary one panelled in with mahogany-stained wood. Look for a toilet with a high-level cistern supported by pretty cast-iron brackets, and a wide, deep basin on a pedestal base, or recessed into a vanity unit. Install a heated towel rail (chrome or brass) on which to hang huge white Turkish towels; if you have a shower, choose an etched glass screen in preference to a plastic curtain. Exchange modern taps for period designs (again in chrome or brass), and plastic shelves and accessories for mahogany ones. See if you can find an antique smoker's chest to hold medicines and toiletries, and, as a finishing touch, add a flower-strewn china dish for soap with its own matching beaker, and a collection of old-fashioned glass scent bottles.

Arts and Crafts

The Arts and Crafts style that first became popular around the end of the last century was characterized not so much by specific design features as by a set of ideas and attitudes that were a reaction against the over-decorated stuffiness of Victorian interiors. Essentially, the movement's followers believed that the appearance of every item should be governed only by its material, its construction and its purpose; each piece should be sturdy, honest and, above all, hand-made, with no superfluous decoration, only exquisitely crafted – and fully exposed – detailing such as mortise and tenon joints. As in medieval times, artist and craftsman were one, and an important part of his role in society was to create useful goods for the common people. Extreme exponents of the theory despised all machines, believing that objects produced with them were lifeless and dead, while any product of hand labour was lively and beautiful.

Although there had been rumblings of similar philosophies for some time, it was the designer William Morris who first translated them into actual schemes and objects, inspired initially by his inability to find any furnishings for his own house that he consi-dered even adequate. Morris was no extremist, though; he was a sensible, intelligent man who understood that machines could be of great value, as long as they were used to assist the craftsman rather than replace him. Despite his perception, however, the theory behind Arts and Crafts furniture was intrinsically ironic, in that the hours of hand labour that went into each item put its price far beyond the reach of the people for whom it was intended. None the less, those who aspired to decorating success could do worse than follow Morris's dictum, 'Have nothing in your house that you do not know to be useful or believe to be beautiful'.

SETTING THE SCENE

William Morris had a strong dislike for clear, pure colour, so an Arts and Crafts scheme should ideally be built around dark, subtle shades such as sage green, russet brown, and Venetian red; if

RIGHT *The billiard room at Wightwick Manor, Staffordshire, decorated by Willian Morris's company in the early 1890s. Hung from a simple brass rail, the curtains are in his Bird design, which has been woven rather than printed. Note the simple lines of the small modern sofa.*

- To complement an Arts and Crafts room, an oriental rug does not have to be of top quality, but it should be old and faded as if coloured with natural, vegetable dyes – a bright, new one would completely spoil the effect. The best places to look for suitable specimens are salerooms, auctions and junk shops, but it's a good idea to have any purchase cleaned before you install it in your home, no matter how pristine it looks.

RIGHT A large collection of oriental blue and white china is displayed against typically muted blue-green panelling in the dining room of Standen, a Sussex house designed by Philip Webb, lifelong friend and colleague of William Morris. Webb also designed the two dressers in the Arts and Crafts style, but the table and reproduction Queen Anne chairs have a more conventionally Victorian look.

this palette is too gloomy for you, however, pick out some of the lighter hues in Morris's designs. Whichever colours you choose, finishes should always be matt rather than glossy.

Although Morris was famous for his wallpaper, he did not altogether approve of it, and saw it as a poor substitute for what he considered to be the ideal treatment – hangings or tapestries. In the absence of these, he recommended covering the walls from picture-rail height to dado with very slightly gathered fabric, plain or printed. Painted panelling in a typically muted colour would also look right, as would plain white walls, but it's important to avoid any sham effects such as graining or marbling.

We now consider polished timber floors to be almost timeless, but in fact they were largely an Arts and Crafts concept; choose either floorboards or parquet tiles, and add oriental rugs. For areas of heavy wear like halls and kitchens, go for stone, or bricks laid in a herringbone pattern, perhaps with traditional rush mats on top.

Arts and Crafts furniture has beautiful proportions, simple lines, chamfered edges and a minimum of carvings; legs are straight, not turned on a lathe or decorated with swirls or claw feet. Typical woods are English – mainly oak, but also walnut, pine, ash, elm, yew and beech, with hinges and mounts of wrought iron or hammered copper.

As in medieval times, textiles – fabrics, rugs, runners, cushions,

• You'll find a huge range of William Morris textile designs in the shops, in several different fabrics and weights: linen union for loose covers and curtains; lightweight cotton for curtains and cushions; and PVC-covered cotton – the modern, easy-care version of traditional oilcloth – for tablecloths. Originally, these fabrics were printed using carved pearwood blocks – a different one for each colour; the same techniques (and in many cases, the same blocks) are still used today to produce a limited range of designs which are very expensive. Fortunately, though, most Morris patterns are now machine printed, and reasonably affordable.

ABOVE RIGHT Morris's wife Janey embroidered this daisy-patterned wool-on-serge hanging, which is now displayed at Kelmscott Manor in Oxfordshire, the couple's country house. The image on the wall is characteristic of the Pre-Raphaelite Brotherhood, an artistic movement that shared many of the Arts and Crafts philosophies.

screens, embroideries and tapestries – were very important. Their designs, whether they were printed, woven, embroidered or stitched, were strictly naturalistic in form and colour, with a strong feeling of growth and movement. The most popular themes were flowers and birds – English species, never exotic ones.

Stained glass windows were common in Arts and Crafts houses, and if you are lucky enough to have one of these, leave it unadorned. Otherwise, choose very simple, sill-length curtains made from plain linen, or a Morris fabric in linen union (a mix of linen and cotton); these should be hung on large rings from a brass or dark wooden pole. For night-time illumination, look for straightforward copper or brass table fittings.

APPLYING THE STYLE
In their quest for a medieval look, Arts and Crafts enthusiasts often installed a high-backed settle softened only by a squab cushion as the main seating. This arrangement won't provide very much

comfort, however, so you'd do better to invest in an ordinary sofa with straight, simple lines, again covered in plain linen or a Morris fabric. As occasional seating, go for one of the chair designs that are closely associated with him as well: the Sussex chair with rush seat and vertical spindles, stained black, red or green, or the eponymous easy chair with padded wooden arms and high upholstered back.

Fix a row of shelves made from wide, thick planks of wood, neatly bevelled at the edges; on these, display copper or brass ornaments that feature obvious hammer marks to demonstrate the hand labour involved in their creation. Try to find one or two pieces of Arts and Crafts pottery, which

BELOW Red House, at Bexleyheath in Kent, was designed by Philip Webb for Morris and Janey when they were first married, and several of the main tenets of the Arts and Crafts style are evident in the design of its upper landing: wooden floors, whitewashed walls and simple, sturdy oak furniture. Through the door at the end of the passage is a typical wooden settle.

had no frilly borders or intricate panels in the prevalent style of the day, but for the first time featured a single, naturalistic motif; alternatively, settle for oriental blue and white china. Flowers should be of the common or garden variety, but in bold hues rather than wishy-washy ones – try wallflowers or Sweet William.

In its existing state, an ordinary Victorian kitchen came very close to exemplifying the movement's principles, simply because it was designed for use, not for show, and its elements were simply crafted in natural materials like wood and stone. In fact, many Arts and Crafts chair designs were inspired by the homely specimens originally intended for use in the kitchen.

Bedrooms should be spare, and dominated by a large bedstead either made from iron or simply carved in wood, which could be hung with fabric at the head only. A large oak wardrobe and chest of drawers plus a matching washstand inset with hand-painted tiles would give just the right look.

When it comes to the bathroom, patterned tiles are very characteristic of this style; the best of these were originally hand-painted by William De Morgan, but there are plenty of good machine-made reproductions around. If you choose decorated tiles, keep the walls plain, but if you opt for ordinary ones, wallpaper in a pale colourway would add interest. Lay ceramic tiles – large ones, or small mosaics – on the floor, or go for warm, practical cork.

- Reproduction tiles in this style are fairly costly, but if your budget is small, don't compromise by using inferior patterned ones throughout; go for plain white, and add pretty border tiles in an authentic design as a finishing touch.

LEFT The Honeysuckle bedroom at Wightwick Manor was named after the pattern of its wallpaper, one of Morris's best-known and most popular. The coverlet and the rug are also his designs, while the spindly rush-seated chair is a signature furnishing item of the style.

Art Nouveau

The Art Nouveau movement led on directly from Arts and Crafts philosophies, but there was one main difference between them; while Arts and Crafts ideas were deeply rooted in the past, Art Nouveau, as its name implies, involved making a clean break with tradition, and seeking out novelty for its own sake. Its main tenets were fantasy and invention, two rather self-indulgent principles that were responsible for the ultimate poverty of the style and the fact that it had come to its end by 1910, barely fifteen years after its birth. Few people could live happily in rooms totally decked out in Art Nouveau, but some of its elements would suit modern homes very well.

Like its predecessor, this idiom took its inspiration from natural forms and colours, but instead of being reproduced naturalistically, these were freely interpreted to the point where they became stylized and distorted, sometimes almost out of recognition. The resulting lines were sinuous, flowing and asymmetrical, so that the shape of an object and its decoration were virtually the same thing. Although Art Nouveau styles sprang up in many countries (including Germany, Italy and Great Britain), and each of them had its own, not always very similar, visual characteristics, it's the romantic, swirly, French version of the style that we usually associate with the term.

SETTING THE SCENE

One of the most important doctrines of Art Nouveau was its insistence that each interior should be planned and furnished as a whole, with everything designed to go together. Often a single motif was chosen to link the different elements in a room – popular ones were insects and flowers, particularly those with bold graphic shapes, like tulips, poppies, lilies and anemones; perhaps the most quintessential motif of all was the peacock feather. A stylized version of this shape would then be sought out as a pattern on curtain fabric, stencilled on the frieze section of the wall, echoed in wrought-iron work, and even set out in tiny mosaics on the floor.

RIGHT On of the most popular mediums for the exuberant Art Nouveau style was stained glass. The same techniques that were used to make colourful, dramatic windows like these were also employed in the manufacture of perhaps the quintessential Art Nouveau accessory – a lamp by Louis Comfort Tiffany.

- Whether your home has an Art Nouveau feeling or not, you could pull any room together with a single motif. Choose a simple, graphic stencil (or cut one yourself), then apply it as a border along the wall at cornice or skirting height – or both. Use it to decorate painted furniture or floorboards, and even blinds and cushions, with the help of special fabric paint. If you're good at needlework, take your motif as the basis for an embroidery or tapestry pattern as well.

- Bentwood furniture is timeless, it goes with lots of different furnishing styles, and it's remarkably inexpensive since it's still mass-produced today using very much the same techniques that were developed in the middle of the last century. Originally adapted from methods used by the shipbuilding industry, these involve treating lengths of wood with heat and steam so they can be bent into the required shapes.

RIGHT *Very different from French Art Nouveau, the work of the Scottish architect Charles Rennie Mackintosh was more angular and upright. This airy, spacious room is in Hill House, a country residence near Glasgow.*

Well-known designers like Charles Voysey and Walter Crane produced typically exotic wallpapers in designs that are still available today, but if you intend to embellish your scheme with lots of Art Nouveau detailing and furnishings, plain walls would provide a better backdrop. This style was heavily influenced by all things oriental, and as a result, woodwork was sometimes painted black, often to blend with ebo-nized furniture. Another frequent feature was a wide shelf at picture-rail height on which a collection of plates or similar ornaments could be displayed.

In furniture making, wood was used as if it were plastic and formed into fluid overall shapes and support structures that frequently echoed the lines of a growing plant; decoration took the form of intricate marquetry and carving.

APPLYING THE STYLE

Art Nouveau chairs and sofas, no matter how preposterous their shape, managed to be less bulbous than mainstream Victorian pieces, yet considerably more comfortable than the unyielding Arts and Crafts settle; a rounded Victorian chesterfield or a serpentine *chaise-longue* would look right. A com- mon accessory (although it was invented several decades earlier by an Austrian, Michael Thonet) was the sympathetically curvy bent- wood chair in one of its many forms – side chair, arm chair or rocking chair.

One bedroom designed by a famous exponent of the style, Emile Gallé, featured a bed whose

ABOVE The flowing forms of this eccentric suite of sofa and chairs take their inspiration from the petals of a flower, while the simple wooden dado panelling and classical column tone down the effect.

head and footboard took the form of giant butterflies inlaid with fruit-wood and mother-of-pearl: those proficient in handling a jig-saw could attempt a simplified version – use turn-of-the-century illustrations as a guide for ideas. Otherwise, go for a carved bed and soft furnishings in a rich, feminine material such as pale damask or velvet, which will help to create a mood of dream-like opulence.

A very important doctrine of Art Nouveau was that the design of everyday household articles could involve just as much creativity as any sculpture or painting, and certainly the individual objects crafted in this style have much more to offer us than any total look. Original items now command a price far beyond the average budget, but it's not difficult to find good-quality reproductions – look for swirling glass vases and bowls that look as if they're made from semi-precious stones; wall and table light fittings whose stands and brackets resemble the stems and tendrils of trailing plants; ornaments and vessels made of silver so smooth it appears to be in liquid form; and stained glass lamps in the unmistakable style of the American designer Louis Comfort Tiffany. If you're not afraid of evoking the era of flower power, adorn your walls with colourful posters by Mucha and Toulouse-Lautrec, whose widespread availability (and therefore popularity) was made possible by contemporary advances in lithography.

RIGHT The exotic romanticism of Art Nouveau furnishings make them ideal for those who want to create a fantasy world in the bedroom. Here, an almost impossibly intricate set of bed and matching wardrobe is balanced by plain white walls and an abundance of space and light. Note the carefully chosen accessories: a softly draping velvet bedcover with matching cushions; typically bulbous, highly decorated cache-pots on equally over-the-top plant stands; and a collection of attractively shaped and coloured foliage.

Art Deco

Art Deco was the first totally machine-age style; its revolutionary shapes, colours and materials successfully merged applied art with industry for the first time, and hugely increased the popularity of mass-produced design.

The age of Art Deco began in Paris in 1925, at the *Exposition des Arts Décoratifs et Industriels Modernes*, whose long-winded title the French quickly abbreviated to the now-familiar term. The look was revolutionary, with its geometric forms – circles, ovals, octagons, straight lines, stepped bases, gentle curves and dramatic zigzags – borrowed from Egyptian, Aztec and American Indian cultures and echoing the Cubist paintings of Picasso and Braque. The new colours (inspired by Leon Bakst's costume designs for the fashionable *Ballets Russes*) were pure, vibrant oranges, yellows, greens and reds, set off by neutrals like black, grey and cream. Even specific motifs in a characteristically stylized version came to be associated with the idiom, most commonly female nudes, closely grouped flowers, attenuated animals (particularly deer), pairs of doves, fronds, spirals, and all manner of sunbursts. It was in its imaginative use of modern materials, however,

that Art Deco made its greatest impact; instead of polished timber, furnishings and accessories were made from plywood (often given a lacquer-like shine with several coats of gloss paint), chrome, plastics like Bakelite, Xylonite and Perspex, and glass, which had recently become available in a strengthened plate version suitable for tabletops and shelving. The design of all types of furniture was dominated by the manufacturing process, and surface decoration was more likely to take the form of large slabs of tinted mirror than fiddly carving.

SETTING THE SCENE

To provide a backdrop for the Art Deco look, rooms should have plain coloured walls (ideally cream), and an absence of intricate architectural detailing such as cornices, picture rails and dados. Instead of small collections of pictures and prints, hang one or two dramatic murals or panels; if you

RIGHT *This ordinary terraced house has been given more than a touch of Art Deco chic by the use of blond wood and geometric shapes. Subtly reinforcing the look are a collection of female images (a typical theme of the style), including a framed sheet-music score from the period.*

- Use modern vinyl tiles to give your hall or kitchen a unique Art Deco floor with a diagonally striped, zigzag or chequerboard pattern; if you have the confidence, you could even make a sweeping curve by cutting the tiles into the required shape. Plan out your design on graph paper before you start, and limit it to cream or white plus one other colour for best results – black is always a safe choice.

- If you're fixing a shelf (or shelves) in the middle of a wall rather than in an alcove, round off both front corners gently to give an Art Deco look and get rid of potentially dangerous protrusions at the same time. To echo the shape of a stepped pyramid, graduate a row of shelves so they increase in size from top to bottom.

RIGHT Once unfashionable, Art Deco pottery is now costly and highly sought after. This tea set exhibits not only an archetypal orange and black colour scheme, but also two characteristically graphic forms – a triangle and a zigzag – in the body and the handle of each piece. Another common Deco motif is the harlequin; here, two are perched dolefully on top of a globe-shaped table light.

can find them, large, circular wall-hung mirrors, or reproduction advertising, travel and railway posters, would also add an authentic touch.

Floors should be pale, so go for 'blond' timber, topped with bold rugs in typically geometric shapes or patterns – no fringes or border designs. Alternatively, lay cream, white, grey or pale beige carpet fitted wall-to-wall, or in the form of a square in the middle of the room, with a contrasting border around it of either carpet strips or painted timber. Kitchen and bathroom floors would originally have been covered with linoleum, but modern vinyl in sheet or tile form looks very similar.

Because of the advances in glass-making techniques, it became possible for buildings to have huge picture windows, and these were usually hung with simple floor-to-ceiling curtains, often extending across an entire wall, and without tie-backs, pelmets or border decoration; for the right feeling choose pale, plain materials.

APPLYING THE STYLE

In the living room, provide seating in the form of chunky sofas with rounded or fluted backs, or curvy, chromium-framed ones in the Odeon style, then add one or two generously sized club chairs or smaller tub designs; moquette, cotton velvet and linen are all suitable upholstery fabrics. To add an authentic touch, try to find an example of that innately Deco furnishing item, the cocktail cabinet; typical examples were mounted on

a stepped base and faced with tinted mirror tiles; inside, a light came on when the door was opened to reveal a large collection of purpose-made glasses with their unmistakable upside-down cone shape. An equally characteristic Art Deco piece is the hoop-framed trolley made from glass and tubular chrome, which was also used in the storage and dispensing of cocktails; these are widely available in reproduction form.

Another Art Deco area that is well covered in terms of reproductions is lighting: fix semi-circular or fan-shaped wall fittings with frosted glass, and supplement these with table lights, at least one of which should be in the form of a scantily clad lady holding a spherical glass shade aloft.

It was during the 1920s that cigarette smoking became fashionable for the first time, and smart living rooms featured a range of appropriate accessories like ashtrays (table models or those on stands) and cigarette boxes, all embellished with suitable motifs. Other highly desirable articles are any item of Art Deco pottery, especially by Clarice Cliff or Susie Cooper (either be prepared to spend a considerable amount, or try to find an odd saucer in a junk shop), or glass – René Lalique was the master here, with his scent bottles, vases, bowls and ashtrays moulded in the shape of flowers, animals and female nudes. Machine-made plastic ornaments of the time are much more likely to have survived than anything made of glass or pottery, and these are often

available at comparatively affordable prices.

One more example of quintessentially Deco furniture is an expansively mirrored dressing table, which was originally designed to show off the increasingly large range of available beauty products with their newly eye-catching packaging. An ordinary divan bed with a semi-circular headboard would tie the look together nicely.

This era was the first in which separate, purpose-built bathrooms were widely installed for the first time, and all the exuberance of the style was employed in their decoration: walls were clad in marble (or more likely wood or plaster painted to look like marble), sheets of mirror, or black and white tiles fixed in a graphic pattern. Choose huge, white sanitary fittings with a characteristic stepped design, and build in a sunken bath for an extra-luxurious touch. Install taps and accessories in highly polished chrome, and store plain-coloured towels on deep glass shelves supported by matching chrome brackets. Near the basin, fix similar, but narrower shelves on which you can display a collection of toiletries in suitably shaped and decorated boxes and bottles. It's not necessary to invest in expensive, authentic Art Deco items, since many modern manufacturers take inspiration for the look of their containers from this heyday of the packaging designer's art. If you're lucky, you might be able to find a tinted mirror in the shape of a stylized sunburst that is small enough to be fixed over the basin.

LEFT The pyramid-inspired stepped shape that is so much an Art Deco trademark has been used to adorn almost every part of this large, stylish bathroom: the generously sized sanitary fittings, the bath panel and the square alcove in which it sits, the tinted mirror, and even the wall just above the skirting board. At dado level, a subtle zigzag border has been stencilled on the softly washed blue-green walls.

International Modern

Born in the Bauhaus School of Design in Weimar, Germany, in the early 1920s, the International Modern style is the dominant movement of this century, and much of the furniture that was developed then is still being manufactured and sold today – not as blind reproductions from an earlier age, but as the very best contemporary design available.

Like Art Deco, an almost exactly contemporary trend, this one was closely allied with technology, but its look is more pared down, with an almost brutal lack of ornamentation. Rooms are spare, sometimes almost empty, reflecting the often-quoted philosophy of one of the International school's most illustrious exponents, the architect Ludwig Mies van der Rohe, that 'Less is More'. Its numerous and vocal early critics declared the style to be barren, impoverished, inhospitable and impractical, and certainly it had none of the obvious allure of the more cheerful Art Deco idiom, but its qualities have proved to be lasting ones; not only has the movement survived, but new designs are being added to it all the time, each one blending effortlessly with its predecessors.

The purity of the International Style was partly a product of design philosophies very like those of the Arts and Crafts movement (honesty of craftsmanship, integrity of materials etc), but it also had its roots in practical considerations. The First World War changed the daily lives of most people for ever; there were many fewer servants, since they were increasingly being employed in industry, so houses had to be made smaller, more streamlined and therefore easier to look after. There was a huge growth in population, and additional housing needed to be built quickly and economically, with no time or money wasted on fussy architectural detailing.

RIGHT *This white living room with its neutral carpet and absence of clutter is a textbook example of the International Modern style. In the foreground are two Wassily chairs, designed by Marcel Breuer, named after Wassily Kandinsky, and inspired by the handlebars of a bicycle.*

• Original works of art – even contemporary ones – are beyond most people's financial reach, but if you live anywhere near an art school, it might be worth investigating their degree show for prints and pictures you can afford – you may even discover an exciting new talent. Alternatively, employ the tried and true solution of hanging posters, or display a more unusual image by exploring the fabric departments of your local shops – both furnishing and dress fabrics – to find a bold, exciting print that you can stretch over a simple frame, then hang on the wall.

RIGHT The Grand Confort armchairs on the left of this all white and glass interior were designed by Le Corbusier in 1928 on the revolutionary principle that the frame could be on the outside; in the dining area is a matching set of Mies van der Rohe's cantilevered Brno chairs.

The essence of this cool, tranquil look revolves around open-plan spaces that can change form and function in an almost oriental manner; huge, flat, unadorned surfaces; natural colours and materials such as marble, wood, leather and silk; straight-sided geometrical forms; and an over-powering feeling of order and discipline, even down to the smallest details: when he had built the towering glass-walled Seagram Building in New York, for example, Mies van der Rohe insisted that all its venetian blinds were permanently adjusted so they could be fixed in only three positions – up, down and at half-mast – thus ensuring that the exterior view would always be a regular one. The importance of this meticulousness to the International style is clearly illustrated by another one of Mies's famous quotes, 'God is in the details'.

SETTING THE SCENE

Rooms should be large and airy, with plaster or brick walls painted white and left almost bare: only a stunning contemporary print or painting can be allowed to break up the surface and add a rare splash of colour.

Floors should not provide any violent contrast – close-fitting wool carpet in a natural oatmeal colour would be ideal, or choose pale timber with a knobbly-textured rug on top, also in wool. Areas of heavy wear (or entire houses in hot climates) could have a shiny, hard flooring; travertine marble is a popular choice among

architects working in this style, but people with slightly more restricted budgets could settle for white ceramic or vinyl tiles instead. Windows are large, and hung with floor-length curtains in a natural cream or white fabric; alternatively, vertical louvre or metal venetian blinds have the right architectural feeling.

International Modern furniture can be made from laminated wood or plastic, but the most common and characteristic material is chrome-plated tubular steel: the first such item was a chair made by the architect Marcel Breuer in 1925, just one year after the technique of chromium plating was perfected. Another furnishing element that was – and is – well served by designers and architects is lighting; search out classic models like the Tizio table fitting with

BELOW A pretty arrangement of flowers, a plump quilt and a warm-hued sisal carpet prevent this graphic black, white and grey bedroom from looking cold and forbidding. Beside the bed is one of the most popular table lights ever designed – the Tizio.

• To provide practical storage capacity that will blend in with your International scheme, go for a collection of cube-shaped units that have a white finish to match the walls. Whether these are store-bought or home-made, they will accommodate a huge range of items, they can be moved from room to room as they're needed, and, unlike fitted shelving, they can be taken with you easily when you move.

its ultra-sophisticated anglepoise construction, or the marble-based Arco floor model, then provide general illumination by means of recessed ceiling spots. For a dramatic touch, install one or two concealed uplighters.

It's important to limit the number of ornaments and accessories – a cluttered effect must be avoided at all costs. If you can afford it, an exquisite sculpture is ideal, but if not, go for a piece of stunningly simple pottery, a large, sculptural plant, or a generously

massed bunch of identical white flowers jammed into a plain glass or ceramic vase.

APPLYING THE STYLE
One vital element in any International style living room is an enormous sofa, with straight lines, a deep seat, a low back and wide, square arms; look for upholstery fabric in natural wool, cotton or silk, and don't be tempted to pile scatter cushions on top. Since an enormous amount of twentieth-century design creativity has been

ABOVE LEFT Geometric shapes and natural materials are essential for the International Modern look. Here, a square theme is carried through from the window panes, to the painting, to the bookshelves, to the tiles on the hearth. In front of the leather sofa, a pure wool rug has been laid over the timber floorboards.

ABOVE One design theory maintains that a white kitchen is the most practical and hygienic because you can see – and therefore deal with – even the smallest amount of dirt immediately. In this almost clinical scheme, the only flashes of colour come from the broad-leaved plant and the collection of cookery books.

devoted to the form of the chair, there is a huge range of occasional seating to choose from: try to find at least one specimen with a cantilevered frame instead of legs, such as Breuer's Cesa chair, which has been in almost constant production since 1928, and is in the collection of the Victoria and Albert Museum. Chairs like these, with their leather, cane or canvas seats, are undoubtedly expensive, so reconcile yourself to having only one or two, or search out some of the excellent copies available.

Many modern fitted kitchens suit this style perfectly – look for a neutral-coloured range with sleek lines, a smooth finish and minimal detailing, then add architect-designed cutlery, cookware, china and appliances, remembering that there can be few seriously trendy kitchens the world over that do not feature one of Michael Graves' classic Alessi kettles.

In the bedroom, install a run of unobtrusive fitted units to cope with clothing and grooming paraphernalia. Transform an ordinary divan bed into an appropriately low platform by stashing away pillows during the day, and fitting it with a tailored cover in natural linen or wool.

Bathrooms should have a similarly pristine, almost clinical feeling; consider a stylish but still infinitely practical scheme of white fittings, with matching white ceramic tiles on both the floor and the walls.

BELOW As the colour of cleanliness and purity, white is also perfect for bathrooms: the only softening touches here are a spray of blooms, a dish of creamy soaps and a polished timber towel rail. To maintain the linear feeling, the shower curtain has been concealed behind a venetian blind.

NEW HORIZONS

Without being tied to any way of life, geographical area or historical period, ideas for beautiful and inviting rooms can spring simply from the imagination of their owners. It's important to remember that, in our time as in any other, only fresh new perspectives can create a unique and memorable contemporary style that will, in its turn, offer inspiration to people of future generations who care about their homes.

Decorator

*M*odern or traditional, exotic or understated, rooms that aspire to the decorator look have as their main characteristics coordination and attention to detail. Unlike the more casual country-house or cottage rooms, these are carefully planned and highly designed, with every element making a significant contribution to the finished effect.

Essentially, this style is concerned with fashion – these schemes are fresh and lively ones in which you can use all the latest tricks and techniques, colours and patterns. It is, however, worth keeping in mind that, by definition, decorator rooms tend to look dated fairly quickly, so be prepared to revamp them completely from time to time.

Fabrics play a significant part in creating this look; apart from major soft furnishing elements such as curtains and upholstery, and minor ones like cushions and tablecloths, they can add interest in the form of piping, borders and appliquéd motifs – even lampshades, covered rubbish bins and desk accessories. Fortunately, creating stunning, risk-free decorator effects has been made much easier over the past few years by the increased availability of fully co-ordinated fabric ranges.

TRADITIONAL STYLE

In any home, the walls offer the largest available surface for adornment; for a really dramatic effect (and a perfect camouflage for irregularities), hang plain or printed fabric, either straight or gathered. Specialized paint effects like dragging, stippling, sponging or ragrolling are equally stylish, but considerably less costly; use them in the kitchen on ageing (or new, but boring) units to tie them in to your scheme. Many fabric ranges include matching or co-ordinating wallpapers, and these will also give the right pulled-together impression.

Another potential area for great design creativity is windows: choose curtains with extravagantly fringed swags, straight or gathered pelmets, or intricately shaped lambrequins – flat, fabric-covered pelmets that extend part-way down the side of the frame. Go for unusual headings like smocking or

---

RIGHT Like a stage set, a decorator-look room demands careful planning and co-ordination for all its elements, whether large or small. In this fashionably stripey town house, even the pictures, the pottery, and the 'flowers' in the hearth have been chosen to tone in the with the fresh cream/blue/tangerine scheme.

- Covering your walls with fabric can add warmth and interest to many different schemes, and there are several different ways to do this. If your material is to be hung straight, you'll have to stitch the widths together first, but if it's to be gathered, the neat selvedges will be concealed in the folds.

- Hem separate widths of fabric at top and bottom, then gather them on to stretchy wires like those used for net curtains.

- Tack your fabric on to wooden battens fixed at cornice and skirting level.

- Clip fabric into place using a purpose-made system of plastic or metal tracks that allows you to take it down for cleaning.

- Fasten fabric directly into the plaster with a staple gun. This is the easiest method, but the least flexible.

- In an *en suite* bathroom, make a shower curtain in one of the materials you have chosen for your bedroom scheme, then back it with a plain clear or white PVC one.

extra-deep pleats, or try a cut away effect like scallops or zig-zags. As a final touch, investigate the full range of trimmings such as piping, flat, frilled or pleated borders, padded or ruffled hems, or tie-backs of cord or fabric, again twisted, pleated or plaited. Another pretty idea is to use a lightweight printed fabric to re-place standard curtain lining. If you want a change from ordinary paired curtains, fix a single one right across the top of the frame, then pull it dramatically to one side with a length of cord: this is called a 'reefed' curtain. Another window treatment that is closely associated with this style is the festoon blind, perhaps with a contrasting frilled border and its own swagged pelmet.

In your bedroom, make elabo-rate drapes for your bed, plus a valance (perhaps a double one with lace underneath) and co-ordinate these in fabric and in style with the curtains or blinds at the window; you could even add a domed canopy or a length of material gathered into a corona over the head of the bed, then draping romantically at each side. On a smaller scale, go for a shaped, padded headboard that matches your bedcover.

You could also try dressing occasional tables to co-ordinate with your windows. To do this, cover any available specimen with a full-length cloth, again with a frilled, pleated or padded hem; if there are lace net curtains at the window, drape the table with an underskirt in the same material,

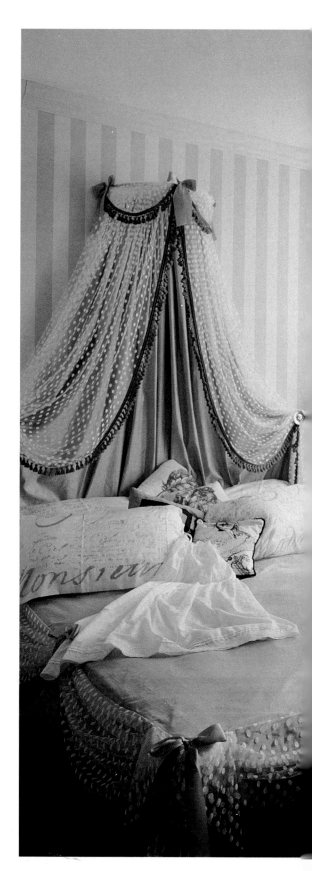

LEFT *Take traditional ideas and shapes, and use them in an exciting new way. The seeds of this romantic ice-blue scheme were sown in the eighteenth century, but witty modern textiles and post-modern furniture bring it right up to date. Linking all the elements is a leitmotiv of bows – catching up the pelmets, adorning the tablecloths, anchoring the swag on the bedcover and adding interest to the layered corona. This degree of design discipline involves making some sacrifices – flowery pink pyjamas must be banished for ever.*

● You can achieve a huge range of decorative effects with cushions: if you're handy with a needle, put together a collection with interesting borders – flat, frilled, scalloped, fringed, padded etc. If sewing is not one of your talents, make simple covers by cutting out and hemming two squares of fabric the same size as your pad. Stitch a length of ribbon to each corner, and in the middle of each side, then tie the squares together with the pad inside. Similarly, cut out and hem one square whose sides are twice as long as those of your pad. Again, stitch ribbon to each corner, then place the pad in the centre of the square with its corners pointing toward the middle of each side of the square. Now tie each corner to the one opposite.

RIGHT A range of co-ordinating fabrics has been used as the basis of this conventionally traditional bedroom. To the right of the window, a collection of patterned plates has been displayed on tiny, individual shelves fitted into a shallow corner.

FAR RIGHT At the other end of the room, the scheme's main colours have been picked up in the throw cushions and the bold, contrast-painted, moulding.

then add a top cloth in the curtain fabric, perhaps caught up at regular intervals with bows or rosettes to expose the lace. If the curtains have cord tie-backs, draw a length of the same cord around your cloth half-way down to give a waisted effect.

Sofas and chairs, too, can be given a 'dressed' look by fitting loose covers with frilled or pleated valances and contrast piping, then piling on co-ordinating cushions. Cover mis-matched dining chairs with full-skirted 'frocks' fastened on with simple fabric or ribbon ties and trimmed with pretty bows.

On the floor, go for fitted carpet in a plain shade meticulously matched to one of your scheme's dominant colours, or look for a tiny, subtle all-over print with a floral motif.

● Skilfully arranged tablescapes will add a decorator finish to the plainest room. Give your displays some kind of theme, such as colour, pattern (chequerboard or trefoil, perhaps), material (ivory or glass) or function (magnifying glasses or pill boxes, for example), or build them around a favourite flower or animal (like roses, or frogs). Compose your arrangements carefully, and re-arrange them frequently so they don't become so stale that you and your visitors no longer notice them. Most tables have to serve a practical function as well as a decorative one, however, so be sure to leave plenty of room for cups and glasses.

When it comes to the all-important accessories, don't skimp on money or imagination: search out large, beautifully shaped table lamps and top them with fabric shades – pleated, gathered or plain, made from pastel-coloured silk or from one of the pale-coloured and lightweight materials used elsewhere. In one corner of the bedroom or living room, install a fabric-covered screen – flat with a shaped top, or gathered on to a carved or painted frame. Instead of using white or cream card, mount a collection of related pictures on squares of whatever wallpaper, fabric or paint effect they are to be displayed against; give them pretty gilded or painted frames, then hang them from ribbon, cord or fabric bows.

One essential element of this style is the tablescape: a carefully chosen collection (definitely *not* a jumble) of ornaments and objects set out like a still-life painting to provide yet another focus of interest and attention.

MODERN STYLE

The modern decorator look is all about breaking with convention, ignoring the 'rules', and creating rooms with an element of surprise. Use traditionally clashing colours like red and pink, blue and green, or lilac and turquoise, and introduce unexpected combinations of materials like chintz and wool, or silk and leather. Cover antique or reproduction furniture with bright modern prints, or use old-fashioned fabrics like damask and brocade in brilliantly fashionable

LEFT Poppies are the order of the day in this warm, inviting dining room – big ones on the table, the cushions and the curtains, and small ones on the wall. Soft furnishings provide decoration in the form of a solid-colour undercloth, a piped, pleated border on the cushions, and a neat geometric heading on the reefed curtain.

hues on chairs and sofa with sleek contemporary shapes.

Walls should be solidly coloured, but instead of paint, go for felt or hessian in bright primary or rich jewel colours: both these fabrics are available with a paper backing especially for this purpose. For a smart touch, frame the walls with strips of contrasting braid or tape fixed along the skirting and cornice, and around doors and windows.

On the floor, lay carpet, again in a small print (geometric this time) or a strong colour that ties in with your scheme. Borders are an important feature of this style, so choose carpet tiles if you want a band of contrasting colour around your room.

Window treatments should be bold and graphic, like crisp Roman blinds or straight curtains; experiment with geometrically quilted fabric in a solid hue and, again, add a colourful border that picks up one of your accent colours. Here, too, you can relate your bed to the window covering by adding a straight canopy and ungathered drapes. Cover one or more tables with a close-fitting, tailored cloth made in matching material, that slips into place like a giant, flat-topped tea cosy – or investigate the cost of having your fabric laminated on to a suitably linear-shaped table.

When it comes to accessories, reinforce the atmosphere of drama and surprise: instead of an ordinary table, for example, arrange display items on a clear Perspex box, ideally lit from underneath.

LEFT Modern decorator rooms are full of surprises – realistic marbling inside crisp, black, almost oriental panels; contemporary pottery on an old, real-marble, fireplace; a serious Le Corbusier chaise-longue next to a fantasy fabric; and a Victorian-style pedestal table given a subtly washed finish of cool sea-green. The style's giveaway characteristics are still there though – the compulsively matched colour scheming and the insistence that every detail blends in perfectly.

High Tech

*C*oined to describe a marriage of high style with technology, the term high tech refers to furniture and accessories that have been removed from their original industrial or commercial context and made use of in a domestic setting. Sturdy, practical, good-looking, and often inexpensive as well, many of these are classic designs whose appearance hasn't changed for decades, so there's little danger of their going out of fashion in a hurry.

CREATING THE LOOK

A high-tech scheme is made up of mainly neutral colours, especially white and black, with pure primaries for accent, plus lots of shiny metal and glass. The most appropriate background is probably white painted walls; grey would work too, but it has a faint air of last year's trend about it. Floors should be hard: go for factory-like boards, plain white or black vinyl tiles, or perhaps the most characteristic of all high-tech surfaces – studded rubber flooring. Those who prefer a warmer surface underfoot could install flat-pile industrial carpet, which is sometimes sold off second hand after being used at a trade fair or exhibition. To give the right feeling, there should be a distinct lack of soft furnishings and draped fabrics, so hang metal venetian blinds or vertical louvres at the windows.

SOURCES OF SUPPLY

One of the richest, and most easily accessible, hunting grounds for adaptable furnishings is an office supply shop; begin with small items like desk lights; stacking filing baskets (excellent for make-up and toiletries, belts and gloves, or little bottles and jars in the kitchen); or small metal rubbish bins (to act as planters for tree-like specimens or to hold toys, shoes or magazines). Once your imagination has been captured, consider larger things like low-level filing cabinets for clothes or kitchen equipment (span two with a sheet of plywood or laminate to make a dressing or kitchen table); typist's chairs for the dining or bedroom; metal lockers for clothing or cleaning equipment; and large, flat designers' plan chests for household linen. A high, dome-topped

---

RIGHT The stark white walls and grey industrial carpeting in this lofty warehouse flat provide a perfect backdrop for the uncompromising furnishing style of a car-freak: sofas made from automobile seats and small occasional tables that are actually hub caps.

• Give a new look to old, slightly battered filing cabinets, lockers, rubbish bins, or anything else made of metal, by treating them to a fresh coat of car spray paint. This is reasonably cheap, it's easy to use, and it comes in a mind-bogglingly comprehensive range of colours to suit any scheme. As a bonus, it will also offer protection from rust if you follow the instructions on the can and prepare the surface carefully. Keep in mind, however, that the fumes from this paint are toxic, so it's a good idea to do your spraying outside on a fine day, or at least in a very well-ventilated room.

RIGHT To gain extra storage capacity that is cheap, roomy and cleanly designed, install one of the metal lockers intended for use in offices and factories. A grey, black and white colour scheme is always a good choice when you want a high-tech look.

waste container is much easier to use than a flimsy pedal bin, and it holds considerably more as well. If your budget is tight, investigate one of the many outlets for used office supplies.

Equipment and materials meant for use in factories can also work very well in the home: look for a heavyweight metal storage system designed for warehouse use that bolts together in sections. This would not only make excellent shelving for books and records, but could also provide the framework for a space-saving platform bed. A tough steel work bench could make a perfect table or desk, while a length of plastic-coated chain link fencing will act as a subtle room divider (and a frame for climbing plants), or serve as the basis for a hanging storage system in the kitchen or bedroom. Instead of ceramic tiles, line your bathroom walls with easy-to-clean corrugated aluminium or sheets of stainless steel, which is also good for the top of a work surface in the kitchen. Industrial lighting adapts well for home use too: hang a metal factory shade over your dining or occasional tables, or fix no-nonsense bulkhead lights in a hall or children's room.

Look in the telephone directory for your nearest catering supply company, most of which are prepared to sell to the public in small quantities. If you cook for a large family, you'll appreciate jumbo-sized, efficiently designed pots and pans, extra-capacity small appliances like toasters, and hard-working, gimmick-free utensils,

ABOVE RIGHT *For maximum practicality and good looks, face walls, storage units, splashback and appliances with satin-finish stainless steel in the style of a restaurant or hospital kitchen. Here, a neat drop-in sink made from the same material leaves the work surface completely clear, and a high-level glass storage shelf makes use of otherwise wasted space. To prevent the room from appearing too industrial and unwelcoming, warm-looking timber boards have been laid on the floor.*

all of which have refreshingly clean lines and undecorated surfaces. Search out simple, practical glassware, crockery and cutlery there as well, plus hard-to-find accessories like a good pepper mill and an effective ice-bucket. On a large scale, replace your domestic refrigerator with a glass-fronted commercial one, or your small cooker with a catering model.

Those who aren't squeamish can obtain a wealth of useful items from a hospital or laboratory sup-

ply company. Glass dressing jars and petri dishes, for example, are great for kitchen storage; test tubes and beakers make stylish vases, and the wire baskets meant for sterilizing instruments and jars can be adapted for storage. The special, extra-sensitive taps that are plumbed in high above the basin and turn on with the flick of an elbow work wonderfully in a domestic bathroom or kitchen, but some water authorities don't allow them in ordinary homes, so check before you buy. Finally, a hospital trolley can be put to excellent use all over the house: in the kitchen (for seldom-used appliances or equipment), in the living room (for serving drinks), in the bedroom (for make-up) and in a home office (for files and books).

Once you get into the habit, you'll be able to find alternative uses for lots of items: wicker or wire bicycle panniers, for example, will hold post in the hall, packets in the kitchen, and bottles in the bathroom. The sort of stacking or folding chairs you find in church halls and school auditoriums might come in handy for parties, while a shop display hanging rail makes an instant, and very cheap, wardrobe – to conceal the clutter, hide it behind a smart screen. Sleek, silvery umbrella lights from a photographer's shop will transform the most ordinary room, and a ship's chandler could yield up a wealth of useful materials like rope and canvas.

LEFT More stainless steel, this time in the form of a sleek, capacious bath and integral towel rail. This tiny but extremely elegant room has walls and floor of pale marble that expand the space visually by providing an unbroken sweep of background colour and texture. Sponges are stored in a laboratory glass cylinder, while a tiny porthole window and a wall-fixed rope basket add a witty, nautical touch that keeps the scheme from taking itself too seriously.

Theme Rooms

*I*nstead of (or possibly in addition to) decorating your rooms in an established style, give them a unifying theme: a colour, a shape, a pastime, or even a city can provide plenty of inspiration and fire your imagination.

COLOURING YOUR IDEAS

One of the most popular starting points for any decoration scheme is colour: one on its own, a favourite combination, or sometimes a family of colours like pastels or primaries.

A subtle, pretty treatment, but not an easy one to bring off, is a monochrome scheme. If this is your choice, it's important that you select your hue – say, a clear blue – and stick to only lighter or darker values of it rather than getting sidetracked into other more greeny or purplish blues, which will ruin the cohesive effect. Add interest by looking for lots of different textures like smooth porcelain or rough knobbly wool, and making sure there are large areas of neutral colour – a timber or coir matting floor, perhaps, or a collection of cane furniture. The ultimate monochrome room is one done out entirely in white, a fashion first popularized by the well-known decorator Syrie Maugham in the 1930s.

Two-colour schemes are another popular choice: black and white ones are classic, but white works just as well with any other colour, as does cream. For a bolder look, go for blue and yellow, or pink and green.

You will usually achieve a harmonious result by using groups of colours that are related in intensity: soft pastels blend beautifully, and bright primaries spark each other off, as long as there is plenty of white for balance. In seldom-used rooms, you could even go for brilliant day-glo tints like shocking pink, lime green, acid yellow and tropical orange.

NATURAL SELECTIONS

Floral themes are not unusual, but it might be fun to take the idea further than printed wallpaper and fabric: display fresh, dried or silk flower arrangements, and supplement these with flower-strewn bowls of fragrant pot-pourri. Stencil individual blooms on to furniture and accessories, stitch

RIGHT This beamed cottage room has been given a sympathetic, but bang up-to-date black and white scheme with carpet tiles laid in a chequerboard pattern, ticking upholstery, and subtle stencilled detailing.

• A stunning all-white scheme can be interpreted to give the impression of austerity or luxury, and adapted for use in a modern, hard-working kitchen or bathroom (using glossy laminate and shiny ceramic tiles), or an old-fashioned bedroom or living room (think of crunchy cotton lace, crisp linen and soft velvet). It's important to remember, however, that the effect will be completely ruined if any of the furnishings is allowed to get even a little grubby, so be prepared to invest considerable time and effort in keeping your room looking pristine.

RIGHT An unbounded enthusiasm for the neo-classical style is reflected in the design of this comfortable living room. As well as the architectural prints on the walls, there are also suitably patterned panels and borders, and a pair of column-shaped lampbases. Although the furniture itself is more curly and French than neo-classical, its arrangement is appropriately formal and symmetrical.

needlepoint or embroidery cushions with floral motifs, and hang pressed-flower pictures on the wall. As a finishing touch, look for Art Nouveau lamps in the shape of stemmed flowers, or settle for petal-shaped shades. If you'd like something a little more unusual, birds, butterflies, fruit, foliage and seashells would also make good starting points for a theme room.

PRINTS AND PATTERNS

Take a favourite motif and see how many ways you can adapt it for use in your room. If bows appeal to you, for instance, start in the obvious way with a suitably patterned fabric or wallpaper, then replace the rings on a lightweight curtain with loops of prettily tied cord or ribbon, and make tie-backs to match. Trim cushions and lampshades with matching or contrasting bows, and anchor the seat pads on your dining chairs with large floppy ones. In a similar way, you could use stars or hearts as your starting point.

Geometric forms lend themselves to lots of furnishing ideas: if you're drawn to a crisp grid shape, choose a carpet that features it, checked fabric for curtains and covers, and ceramic tiles fixed with contrasting grouting to reinforce the effect. Look for a wire grid storage system, and square tables topped with glass that has been reinforced with a grid-shaped pattern of wire; you could even conceal ugly high-level pipework by installing a false ceiling of separate pieces of timber laid across each

BELOW Fish, fowl and game provide the decorative details in this kitchen, with a well-stocked stream running along the splashback, and gambolling creatures on the blind, the pottery and the window's tiled reveal.

FAR RIGHT Rough, sandy walls and brilliant sunlight conjure up the exotic allure of the African desert in this bathroom. The earthy colours of the landscape are echoed in the stone floor, the textiles and pottery, and the richly patterned towels.

other in squares. Most other shapes could be adapted in similar ways: think of circles, triangles or just plain stripes.

Successful schemes can also be built around traditional patterns such as tartan and paisley; once again, don't stop at the obvious things like textiles, but see if you can find (or make) lots of small objects that will link in as well.

DECLARING AN INTEREST

If your life is dominated by a particular sport or hobby, let your room reflect it. Keen sailors, for example, could cover their seating with sailcloth or canvas, tie back their curtains with nautical rope (embellishing the ends with decorative knots instead of tassels), clad their walls with timber fixed horizontally to look like shiplap, and hang round mirrors that resemble portholes. Without taking the theme quite so far, you could cater for almost any pastime – sports, theatre going, train spotting, music making – simply with pictures, prints and accessories.

- A few sheets of plywood and a little paint can transform a child's bed into a magical place, so copy simple cartoon drawings to make a frame that looks like a car, a boat, a train engine or a rocket ship.

RIGHT Suggest a fifties American diner by choosing an appropriate pink, red and black colour treatment and adding seating in the form of leatherette banquette, chrome chairs and swivelling stool. The boomerang-shaped motifs on the curtains are absolutely typical, as are the metal Venetian blinds.

FAR RIGHT The sky's the limit in this charming child's room, whose walls and door panels have been softly washed with blue, then hand painted with clouds, kites and rainbows. When night falls, a friendly man-in-the-moon lights up to keep scary monsters at bay.

TIMES AND PLACES

Choose a recent period for inspiration, like the fifties, which can be interpreted in a fairly free way: look for black wrought iron furniture that has splayed legs with coloured balls on the ends; grey metal venetian blinds; boomerang-shaped tables; and furniture covered in vinyl patterned with bright pink or turquoise and black motifs. The forties or the sixties – even, terrifyingly, the seventies – can offer similar scope.

If you have a favourite city, collect and display things that remind you of it, including travel posters and large-scale souvenirs like a model of the Eiffel Tower or the Chrysler Building.

SMALL CHANGES

Theme rooms are perfect for children, and their passions can prove an endless source of inspiration: consider re-creating a zoo, a farmyard, an aeroplane, a space-station, or a submarine. Take your child's favourite story or character – anything from Peter Rabbit to Postman Pat – and use it as the basis for a large mural, or a series of small stencilled pictures on walls, blinds or painted furniture.

Bizarre and Eccentric

You can have enormous fun creating and living in a room whose style is pure fantasy, and whose only limitations are those of your imagination. Take care, though, in deciding which rooms you want to treat this way, and how far you're prepared to go. Young people with their first – perhaps one-room – home are sometimes tempted to dream up a totally anarchic scheme that differs dramatically from the cosy, traditional one they associate with their parents, but a small-space dwelling is often the least appropriate for an over-the-top treatment: an environment you create to stimulate, and perhaps even shock, can quickly become irritating when you spend most of your time in it, and especially when you feel ill or depressed. Remember, too, that you may be entertaining friends of widely varying ages and tastes, and you'll want everyone to feel comfortable and at ease; by all means, add witty touches and unexpected colours, but try to bring your more extravagant fantasies down to earth. Like strong colours, surreal schemes are best suited to rooms that aren't used very often, or for very long, like bathrooms (particularly second bathrooms), guest rooms, separate dining rooms, or to a slightly lesser extent, halls and bedrooms.

LOOKING FOR IDEAS

Try a modern pastiche of the classical idiom with a *trompe-l'oeil* treatment for the walls that looks like crumbling columns, or use stencils to adorn them with rows of urns or a Greek key motif; in a similar vein, paint the floor to look like marble or mosaic tiles. Provide seating in the form of low divans heaped with cushions, and add several 'sculptures' in fibreglass or plastic – museums often sell suitable ones. In a bathroom, choose white fittings with column-shaped supports, and install a sunken bath. Cover the

---

RIGHT The paintings of Henri Matisse provided the inspiration for this vibrant, exciting room. If you're nervous of anything other than safe, neutral shades, begin by introducing bright, pure colours in the form of paint or accessories that can easily be replaced if you don't like them.

- For a good selection of stone 'furnishings', check out your local garden centre: a backless bench could act as a coffee table, for example, while a tall column would make an excellent plant stand. Instead of classical sculptures, dot decorative stoneware figures around, and keep magazines and newspapers in a large, urn-shaped tub.

walls with real mosaic tiles; alternatively, create a classical mural on a wall or, using fabric paint, on a roller blind.

Fulfil an eastern fantasy by hanging your walls with opulently coloured fabric, gathered from the top only and falling loosely at the hem. Make a tented ceiling in matching material, and cover the floors with layered carpets and rugs, topped with piles of richly embroidered and patterned floor cushions in deep hues like purple, gold and wine red. Search out an array of brass accessories like

lamps and trays, and drape windows, tables, chairs and sofas with shawls, rugs or fabric in suitable colours and patterns – you can often find printed bed-linen in beautiful oriental designs that is actually cheaper than similar material bought by the metre.

As a complete contrast, go for a ruthlessly minimalist look, which involves taking oriental simplicity to its absolute extreme. To take on this idiom spiritually you have to get rid of most of your possessions, but you can achieve it visually by hiding them away in

RIGHT Create an exotic tent-like effect in your bedroom with a collection of intricately patterned rugs. Here, hand-woven kelims have been spread on the floor, cut up to cover cushions, and used as coverlet, canopy and hangings on the bed. To set off their rich colours and knobbly texture, choose bedlinen made from smooth white cotton.

FAR RIGHT The design framework of this transformed suburban room was created easily and cheaply using pale striped wallpaper, coir matting, lengths of unstitched muslin and medium density fibreboard for the unusual arched and curved display alcove. The room's focus however, is the unique triangular dining table and co-ordinating chairs; you might be able to commission a similarly sculptural piece from one of the furniture design degree students at your local art college.

● Large sheets of mirror are very difficult for an amateur to install, they're extremely expensive to replace if you break them in handling, and they can pose a serious safety hazard, so if you're not an expert, go for small mirror tiles instead, which are available with an adhesive backing that makes them comparatively easy to handle and fix. Unless your wall is unusually flat, you'll need to cover it with a sheet of plywood or chipboard so the image reflected in the tiles isn't distorted by bumps in the plaster.

RIGHT A liberal sprinkling of 'ormolu' accessories, a dramatic sweep of burnished golden fabric and a collection of needlepoint textiles are displayed against a background of elaborate trompe-l'oeil architectural detailing to turn this fairly ordinary room into a rococo fantasy. Note the confident addition of contemporary designs like the sunny yellow teaset and the large fruit bowl with its almost primitive rose motifs.

capacious cupboards built floor to ceiling: fit flush doors that have a press-open mechanism instead of handles, which only interrupt the pure surface. Walls and floors should be plain and bare, unsullied by picture or rug, and certainly not cluttered with skirtings or cornices; colours are black and white, with perhaps the odd splash of grey. Any object not in current use should be concealed, including mattresses, tables and chairs, but each room can have one exquisite object like a flower or a piece of sculpture, that provides its focus of interest. This look can be greatly saving of money, but not of time or effort, since surfaces that are so mercilessly exposed must be absolutely flawless.

In a more frivolous vein, take Art Deco style over the top by creating a Hollywood fantasy room with peach-tinted mirror covering a whole wall, heart-shaped cushions in gold and silver, leopard-print upholstery, and silky curtains. In a bedroom, install an elaborate dressing table with light bulbs all around the mirror, film-star fashion, and find satin-look polyester sheets for the bed.

Experiment with a grand rococo theme, using lots of ormolu-ish gold paint, papier-mâché swirls, cut-out or painted-on cherubs, and seating covered in pink or blue brocade; alternatively go for an artistic style with huge abstract murals in garish colours, intense decoration on every available surface, and an extensive collection of pottery, pictures and generally aesthetic clutter.

Eclectic

*M*ost real, lived-in rooms, now and throughout history, could accurately be described as eclectic ('borrowing freely from various sources' – *OED*), since few of us ever have the opportunity to start with a completely empty space and enough money to furnish it fully. Victorian rooms, therefore, had lots of Georgian things in them, and Georgian ones contained plenty of elements from earlier centuries. In our age more than most, however, there seem to be no restrictions at all on combining antiques of widely differing periods with each other and with modern pieces, so a few guidelines are needed if the result is to be an interesting and stylish mix, rather than an unsightly muddle.

MIXING AND MATCHING

It's probably wise to wait until you've developed a certain degree of confidence and a reasonably educated eye before you attempt to combine very disparate elements: once you've established certain qualities that appeal strongly to you – colours, shapes, details – these will themselves give some unity to your schemes. Do a little bit of research into your favourite styles to find out why they developed as they did, and what the philosophies are behind them; this kind of information is not only very interesting, it will also help you by making it clear which idioms have guiding principles in common. For example, the Arts and Crafts movement is based on ideas very similar to those of the International Modern school, so it makes sense that solid, honest Arts and Crafts items will not jar with straightforward, unadorned Modern ones. For the same reason, spare oriental things would go well with either of these styles, but typically Victorian furnishings, with their emphasis on surface decoration and curvy shapes, would not. Early English furniture might also look odd with Georgian or Victorian specimens, but, again, would sit happily next to a Bauhaus chair or sofa. Primitive or ethnic artefacts need a suitably austere setting, so here again, don't try to fit them into a gentle, chintzy country scheme.

LEFT This dramatic scheme has borrowed elements from several different design idioms: the plump sofa and rug-topped coir matting suggest country living; the cane furniture hints at exotic climes; the marble fireplace adds a period note; and the pottery and pictures represent contemporary craftsmanship.

- It's important to remember that the term 'eclectic' is not just a handy label for a jumble of decorating idioms – it's a look every bit as disciplined as any other. Even before you begin to think about the effect you want to create, make sure you will be working with a genuine and balanced mix of furnishing items – one old-fashioned chair in a modern room (or vice versa) will simply look out of place.

DISPLAY TECHNIQUES

When there is a great deal of tension and drama in a room's furnishings, it's important to keep the background simple and uncluttered, so go for plain walls, unfussy window treatments that don't contrast sharply with them, and timeless, all-over floor coverings such as timber boards, coir matting or neutral-coloured carpet. Pale, traditional hues are the safest choice, but if you like the idea of something brighter and more modern looking, again make sure it will be in sympathy with

LEFT Restrained neo-classical furniture and accessories can be displayed surprisingly successfully with hard-edged twentieth-century designs: note the elegant pieces of Georgian silver (an urn and an oval box) that seem perfectly at home on the marble top of a steel-framed table.

the furniture: a massive oak cupboard from the seventeenth century could look dramatic against a vivid yellow wall, for instance, but a delicate, gilded table would be completely overpowered. Make sure there are several unifying elements – a favourite colour, perhaps, a certain style of table lamp (cream ones with round bases, maybe), or a particular kind of upholstery fabric. Try to ensure that modern services are not too intrusive, since an ugly radiator or a harsh ceiling light could ruin a carefully balanced arrangement. Above all, don't try to crowd in too many things: each item should have enough space around it so that it can be clearly seen and its individual characteristics fully appreciated.

Remember that there is a large element of risk inherent in any eclectic scheme, so have the courage to experiment, and perhaps fail; creating an exciting and very individual room in this way is not easy, but the potential for personal satisfaction is enormous.

ABOVE A wider view of the light, spacious apartment illustrated opposite. Although the windows and the ceiling decorations are Georgian, this large, high area has been divided up sympathetically using an uncompromisingly modern grid device – open for the timber ballustrade in the foreground, and closed on the solid room dividers further back.

189

Index

Index

ACKNOWLEDGEMENTS

The publishers would like to thank the following for their kind permission to reproduce the photographs in this book:

Front and back cover courtesy of Marks & Spencer plc; *8* Tom Leighton/EWA; *10* Michael Boys Syndication; *12* Homes & Gardens/WPN; *13* Warner Fabrics plc; *18/19* Michael Boys Syndication; *20* Woman's Journal/WPN; *21* Michael Boys Syndication; *22/23* Country Living/Dennis Stone; *25, 26/27, 30* Homes & Gardens/WPN; *31, 32/33, 35* Spike Powell/EWA; *36/37* Country Living/Tessa Traeger; *38, 39, 41* Michael Boys Syndication; *42/43* Jon Stefanidis/Fritz von der Schulenburg; *44/45* Country Living/Chris Drake; *46* Smallbone of Devizes; *47* Simon Horn Furniture; *48/49* Camera Press; *51* The Image Bank; *52/53* Richard Bryant/Arcaid; *56/57* Fritz von der Schulenburg; *58* Robert Harding Picture Library; *59, 60/61* The Image Bank; *63* Camera Press; *64/65* Lars Hallen/Design Press; *66* Fritz von der Schulenburg; *67* Camera Press; *71* Gerald Pearce/Fritz von der Schulenburg; *72/73* Options/WPN; *74* EWA; *75* Michael Boys Syndication; *77* Meubles Grange; *78* Michael Boys Syndication; *79* Smallbone of Devizes; *80/81* Bathroom Trading Co.; *83* Options/WPN; *84/85* Camera Press; *86* Homes & Gardens/WPN; *87* Michael Boys Syndication; *88/89* Futon Co.; *91* Country Living/Simon Brown; *93* Mike Crockett/EWA; *97* Homes & Gardens/WPN; *98* Susan Griggs Agency; *99* EWA; *100/101* John Bethell Photography; *102* Art Directors Photo Library; *106/107* Lucinda Lambton/Arcaid; *108/109* Michael Boys Syndication; *110* Michael Dunne/EWA; *111* Homes & Gardens/WPN; *112/113* Michael Boys Syndication; *115* Art Directors Photo Library; *116/117* Spike Powell/EWA; *118/119* Jerry Tubby/EWA; *120* David Cripps/EWA; *121* Spike Powell/EWA; *122/123* World of Interiors/Christopher Simon Sykes; *124* Michael Boys Syndication; *125* Clive Helm/EWA; *128/129, 132/133* Woodmansterne; *135, 136* Christine Bastin & Jacques Evrard; *137* Robert Harding Picture Library; *138/139* Tim Street-Porter/EWA; *141, 143* Spike Powell/EWA; *144/145* BC Sanitan; *147* Tim Street-Porter/EWA; *148/149* Mary Fox Linton/Fritz von der Schulenburg; *150* Homes & Gardens/WPN; *151* Richard Bryant/Arcaid; *152* Rodney Hyett/EWA; *162/163* Osborne & Little; *164/165* Woman's Journal/WPN; *167* Tim Street-Porter/EWA; *168/169* Camera Press; *170, 171* Richard Bryant/Arcaid; *173* Country Living/David Brittain; *174/175* Michael Nicholson/EWA; *176* Homes & Gardens/WPN; *177* Aqua Ware; *178* Tim Street-Porter/EWA; *181* Options/WPN; *182* Country Living/Simon Brown; *184/185* Options/WPN; *187* Woman's Journal/WPN; *188/189* Richard Bryant/Arcaid.

The publishers would also like to thank the following companies for supplying props for special photography:

2/3 sofa fabric, G.P. & J. Baker Ltd, 17 Berners Street, London W1; curtain fabric, Warners Fabrics plc, 7 Noel Street, London W1; green stripe wallpaper, Marks & Spencer plc, 173 Oxford Street, London W1, and branches; lace curtain and pink moiré, The John Lewis Partnership, Oxford Street, London W1, and branches; *68/69* kelim, Graham & Green, 4 & 7 Elgin Crescent, London W11; tiles, The Reject Tile Shop, 178 Wandsworth Bridge Road, London SW6; *154/155* fabric, Timney-Fowler Ltd, 388 King's Road, London SW3.